The Writing Tutor

Marian Arkin
LaGuardia Community College
The City University of New York

Barbara Shollar
College of New Rochelle

Longman
New York & London

The Writing Tutor

Longman Inc., 19 West 44th Street, New York, N.Y. 10036
Associated companies, branches, and representatives throughout
the world.

Library of Congress Cataloging in Publication Data

Arkin, Marian, 1943-
  The writing tutor.

  (Longman series in college composition and communication)
  Supplement to: The tutor book / Marian Arkin, Barbara Shollar.
New York: Longman, c1982.
  Bibliography: p.
  1. English language—Rhetoric—Study and teaching.   2. Tutors
and tutoring.   I. Shollar, Barbara. II. Arkin, Marian, 1943-
Tutor book.   III. Title.   IV. Series.
PE1404.A73   808'.042'071173   82-189
ISBN 0-582-28232-2   AACR2

Manufactured in the United States of America

CONTENTS

VI. TUTORING MECHANICS: GRAMMAR, PUNCTUATION, SPELLING AND FORMAT 66

VII. ANNOTATED BIBLIOGRAPHY 73

ACKNOWLEDGMENTS

Marian Arkin would like to thank writing tutors at LaGuardia Community College; students in peer tutoring classes (1977-80, LaGuardia Community College; 1981, Rhode Island College); and the following colleagues for advice and material: John Roche, Department of English, Rhode Island College; Thomas Nash, Department of English, Auburn University; Beverly Gudanowski, University of Massachusetts, Boston; Marjorie Levenson, Massachusetts Bay Community College, Newton; Steven North, Department of English, SUNY at Albany; Kenneth A. Bruffee, Department of English, Brooklyn College (CUNY); and those at LaGuardia Community College--Doris Fassler, Brian Gallagher, Leonard Vogt, and Harvey Weiner; and Bert Eisenstadt, Mark Prinz, and Enis Swarm of the Writing Center.

For their willingness to experiment, Barbara Shollar would like to thank the writing tutors at the College of New Rochelle, and her students in peer tutoring within the School of New Resources. For the dialogue begun with colleagues in the Writing Program at Herbert H. Lehman College (CUNY), thanks to directors Michael Paul and Robert Carling; and for those times when we carried our dialogue to the West End and shared our ideas about writing and politics and taught our lessons to one another, much thanks to Cynthia Badendyck, Rod Keating, Laury Magnus, Monica Raymond, Karen Robertson, Lawrence Rosenwald, and Richard Russo. Thanks, also, to my colleagues at the College of New Rochelle: Anna Greene, Angel Capellan, Robert Gardener, Annette Zelman, and Isabel Byron, coordinators of writing programs, and Bessie Blake in the School of New Resources, and Kathie Henderson, Director of the Writing Program in the School of Arts and Sciences and the School of Nursing, all of whom shared methods, insights, and experiences which have enriched this text.

Thanks must go to our editor Tren Anderson, whose idea this was initially. We feel especially grateful to Thom Hawkins, Director of the Writing Center, University of California, Berkeley, for the seriousness with which he took our project and the alacrity with which he responded to our work. His review of our manuscript helped immeasurably. Of course, any mistakes and infelicities that remain are our own.

Finally, we owe a particular debt of gratitude to
Charlotte Frede. She learned to read our writing
and make sense of our composing process, willingly
typed our drafts, and otherwise dealt cheerfully with
the trials of dual authorship.

M.A.
B.I.S.
New York City

PREFACE: TO THE WRITING TUTOR

You may be a graduate student, an undergraduate work-study student or intern, a professional staff person or faculty member. You may be part of a writing lab, a multi-disciplinary skills center, or in a program servicing a special group of students. You are a writing tutor, someone trained or in training to help writers at every stage of the writing process.

This pamphlet talks directly to you about the work you do. It provides you with material, resources, and strategies that will enable you to tutor writing more effectively by:

- exploring the underlying structures and approaches common to all written work and

- including specific information, where necessary, to enable you to deal with specialized problems relevant to your particular academic discipline or profession

First, however, we would like to discuss the writing process since we believe your understanding of that process should structure your whole approach to tutoring. Indeed, the way we look at the process of writing provides the rationale for the structure and substance of the pamphlet.

Speech, the Written Work, and the Writing Process

The Relationship Between Speech and Writing   As opposed to writing, in speaking we can use intonation and stress, as well as natural rhythms and pauses to increase clarity.

Moreover, we talk to others and engage in an implied, if not actual, dialogue, that is we rely on visual responses and gestures from others to let us know if we have been clear, or if we need to put something into other words: a puzzled look will signal us to explain our position further, an expression of annoyance will clue us in to changing our tack; a nodding head will let us know we need only keep hammering the point home. Somebody expressing agreement is likely to stimulate us to expand our ideas; another person, taking exception to our position, will force us to produce new arguments. Another person with reasonable reservations may motivate us to take previously unconsidered claims into consideration.

Writing detaches us from this immediate human context and jolts us into developing a whole range of substitutes for the conventions of spoken language. For once our listeners have become readers, a series of strategies must replace the give-and-take of our previous dialogue. That does not mean we talk to ourselves or even pretend to carry on a conversation with someone else, though it can. After all, some such process must be going on in order for us to create a written work. In part, you as a tutor recreate the role of the auditor so your tutees can use the dialogue to improve their writing.

The Written Work   If writing loses some color, vivacity, and warmth in its translation from the spoken word, it nonetheless has its compensations. By comparison, the written language is capable of greater depth and precision; writing allows us to explore an argument or idea in all its complexity while its relative permanence means that readers can give it the careful attention it deserves, scrutinizing it at their leisure. Or it can (re)create activities and events, describing, recounting, and discussing them in loving and fulsome detail. These special strengths and pleasures of the written word are especially in focus in the final form, after all the wrinkles in the writer's logic have been ironed out, once all the capitals have been inserted and the last changes in diction have been made.

What we don't see in the final product are all the false starts, the scrambled sentences and paragraphs, the examples that didn't do quite what they were supposed to, the pretentious or incorrect expressions, not to speak of the dangling participles and lack of agreement between the verbs and several collective nouns—all of which were corrected, or eliminated from one draft to another. However, in our appreciation of the written product, we often forget that writing is a process. Not recognizing that writing is a process may be especially damaging to writers who are vulnerable to thinking that they have to get it all right the first time round.

The Writing Process   Writing is a cultural phenomenon: it is acquired slowly, sometimes painfully, often unconsciously. As a cultural phenomenon, it is conditioned by a variety of circumstances, including physical conditions, psychological attitudes, intellectual resources, emotional elements. The writing process is often seen as a four-part activity: prewriting, composing, revision, and proofreading. <u>Prewriting</u> is the stage in which writers discover and invent the ideas they will use while composing. <u>Composing</u> is the transformation of jotted notes, and schematic diagrams and outlines into drafts and rewrites. In <u>Revision</u> the last of these drafts becomes final: at this stage the writer checks for unity and coherence, refines the style and syntax and corrects grammar. <u>Proofreading</u> is the final pruning and perfecting of all areas. The writing process, in other words, is comprised of successive stages, each of which has characteristic elements. Understanding how these elements function in each stage offers the writer the chance to learn strategies in order to master different conventions involved in producing a written work. One strategy may be more suitable for one stage than for another. For instance, a writer need not really be concerned with the accuracy of the spelling until the proofreading stage. On the other hand, a writer will need to come up with some good arguments for his or her position in one of the early-to-middle stages of writing.

At the outset, then, it may be helpful to make your tutees become more aware of writing as a <u>process</u>. With this awareness, novice writers can begin to think of and see the written work as something that <u>evolves</u> and therefore constantly changes, and, by extension, as something that <u>can</u> <u>be</u> <u>changed</u>. Learning that there are many stages at which writing can be corrected and refined provides the writer with increased control. All writers know how difficult writing can be and poor writers especially know how much of themselves they bare in the effort. What poor or beginning writers often <u>don't</u> know is how many problems they share in common with other writers and how many options are available to them for solving their writing problems. They need to know that the written work is not a static and impervious structure but a constantly evolving one; knowing that, they can begin to see that writing need not be left to chance. You can help your tutees by showing them at which points they already successfully control the writing process (which they often do without thinking) and so help to give them confidence in developing further strategies to control other stages with which they have had difficulty.

Like any model, however, the one for the writing process is an ideal or paradigm: it is not meant to be applied in toto to any individual. Writers must adapt the model to their own needs, and tutors must

3

help writers isolate those strategies and techniques most useful to them. Let us take two examples, one at either extreme of the writer's spectrum. One writer, for example, uses a "prewriting" stage to think through his ideas. By the time he gets to composing, then, he knows exactly what he wants to say. His first draft is very close to the final essay. For this writer, the second draft is more a reviewing, and often, the final one; he uses revision to refine the essay, clarifying syntax, sharpening lexical choices, correcting grammar. For the writer at the other extreme, the first draft of an essay is a stage in which ideas tumble onto the page. Everything that's been churning around during the prewriting stage is released. Some of it stays: much of it is metamorphosized, retaining only the slightest resemblance to the original. Writing for this person is a way of thinking through notions, clarifying them and giving them shape, and, during the succeeding drafts, deciding what she really means to say and how to say it best. It is not rare, then, for this writer to change her thesis one, two, five times before a paper is really finished—to cut and paste, moving whole sections from one portion to another. In each draft, more and more remains—and finally the work is done. To this writer, the writing process is a constant re-seeing.

Most writers fit in between these extremes. It is well to be aware that we write differently and that the strategies we need to use will differ according to the way we work best as writers. It is essential, then, that during tutoring you and your tutee share your different approaches to writing, including any personal idiosyncrasies in writing habits, and compare your processes with the ideal model of the writing process. Your concern as a tutor is to fit the process to the tutee rather than the tutee to the process.

The Writing Tutor's Role

The extent of the tutoring help you give will, of course, depend on the nature of your program and the policy of your lab. Some of you may be encouraged to become involved in collaborative learning and to work with your tutee throughout the entire writing process (finding a topic, developing ideas, deciding structure, etc.); others will be limited to reviewing

4

work that has already been handed in, graded, and, sometimes, returned for revision; many of you will be responsible for tutoring only grammar. Apart from program policy, you yourself will have to consider the fine line that sometimes exists between "going over" students' work and doing it for them and distinguishing a "draft" that represents work "in process" from a revision that is their best effort.

We believe that a knowledge of the overall writing process will be helpful to you no matter what form your tutoring takes. Your role as an auditor is a crucial one: as a sympathetic ear, you will help your student develop positive attitudes toward him- or herself as well as toward writing; as a listener to various drafts, you will be a kind of echo chamber. Reading his or her own work to you, a student is more likely to hear errors and problems of syntax, development, or organization reflected by your presence. As an actual reader, you can give tutees a sense of how writing sounds at every stage of the various drafts. Even work on isolated grammatical elements will become more productive if you can help your tutee put grammar in its proper perspective in the context of the entire process. By reading work aloud, if only at the proof-reading stage, you can dramatically demonstrate how you stumble on an agreement error or an unpunctuated modifier and so help the student to self-correct.

As you develop your tutoring expertise, you should gain a clearer understanding of writing problems. You will learn the terminology ("This is a fragment." "You have a dangling modifier."), but these terms alone will not suffice. You will still need to make sure that students understand what the terms mean and how they apply to the students' writing. Meanwhile you can rely with confidence on the effectiveness of comments you now use such as: "This doesn't make sense to me." "Are you saying....?" and "Do you mean the cat is chairing the meeting?"

What This Pamphlet Contains and How to Use It

This pamphlet begins with assessment, first asking you to analyze yourself as a writer to discover your own strengths and weaknesses as a prelude to helping others do the same. Examining yourself will help you develop your own study program. You can then assess your tutee with more confidence. The Tutee Profile section provides you with material to determine how your tutee can benefit from your tutoring; a writing inventory of your tutee's writing process will help you get the information you will need to tutor him or her most effectively. You can then use this information as the basis for discussing short-term and long-term goals. All these diagnostic strategies will help you and your tutee formulate a Writing Contract (discussed in the Tutee Plan section).

The major portion of the pamphlet discusses the writing process in detail, primarily in terms of strategies, techniques, and methods you can use to help your tutees to strengthen their writing: Section IV focuses (1) on activities to do before writing and (2) on those elements to be emphasized during writing, Section V on revising, while Section VI deals with mechanics. While we recommend you read the entire pamphlet to get an overview, you may also use the last three sections as a glossary to help you find techniques to use with your tutee at any particular stage in the writing process.

For those of you who have been stimulated by your tutoring experience, the Annotated Bibliography will help you to explore various aspects related to language study. Selective, it reflects recent work in the field of composing and the combination of theory and research directly applicable to tutoring. It also includes selected texts you can use in your tutoring.

II. ASSESSMENT

Assessment should be an ongoing activity, for it is integral to all learning. The initial evaluation, however, is the most important, since it establishes a base line to help people set appropriate goals for whatever activity they intend to pursue. What follows are two assessment mechanisms, one for writing tutors and another for writing students. These profiles should allow you to evaluate your own strengths and weaknesses and those of your tutee.

Tutor Profile

Before you begin to tutor, you should find it helpful to ascertain how much you do and don't know about your field. The following profile was prepared to help you assess yourself, that is, to find out what you need to study. After you take the test, review it with your supervisor, course instructor, or fellow tutors who will probably recommend areas in which you need work. Do not get discouraged if a first assessment shows you need to do some serious studying. Your studies will be well reinforced by your tutoring. And your tutoring will provide you with incentive to study. Notice that the profile tries to balance the three aspects we believe most important to good writing: an understanding of one's motives and one's abilities as well as that of others, an awareness of the composing process, and a knowledge of grammar, syntax, and mechanics.

Part One: Essay   Choose from among the following. Your essay should be from 300 to 500 words.

1. Portrait of a Tutor: Describe and explain the qualities of a good tutor. Include here a discussion of the qualities you have and those you would like to develop.

2. Case Study I: A thirty-five-year-old practical nurse has returned to school to complete her B.S. degree in nursing and has been told that her writing does not meet the criteria of academic prose. With an already tight program (since many courses are

7

required) and an already tight schedule (she is con-
tinuing to work to support herself), she is loath
to take a course that is not otherwise required in
her curriculum; she has come to the Writing Lab as an
alternative. Her attitude is somewhat negative and
resentful; she is also pressed for time... Describe
your initial conference with this learner; what would
you need to tell her, and to find out from her. Discuss what goals you think you might establish and
what skills you might work on developing.

3. Case Study II: A student writing a senior thesis
in psychology is required to submit a paper which includes a review of the literature, a discussion of
theory, an experimental model, and its application
in the classroom. He has come to the Writing Center
because the professor has rejected the first draft
because of its lack of organization, inadequate documentation, and lack of proper research format. It is
before midsemester. In your essay, explore how you
would discuss the situation with the student, including the goals you might establish and the skills you
might work on developing.

4. Case Study III: Your student is a high school
dropout who has succeeded in her job but now seeks a
promotion and wishes to improve her writing skill.
She has turned to the Adult Education Center to master
material she will need to obtain a high school equiv-
alency certificate. A sample of her writing reveals
an extensive use of Black English and an ignorance of
mechanical error; it has, however, an interesting discussion of infant nutrition. In your paper, discuss
the goals you might establish and the strategies you
might use with this learner.

Part Two: Writing Description   In writing, answer
the following questions about your essay:
    1.   What is the thesis?
    2.   What are the main points? And how have they
        been developed?
    3.   Who is the audience? (To whom is the essay
        written?)
    4.   What voice or tone is the essay written in
        and why?
    5.   What is the aim in this essay and how has
        the aim affected writing choices? (How is
        the aim consistent or inconsistent with the
        assignment?)
    6.   Describe the process you underwent in coming
        up with the final essay.

ing essay (part of a take-home final in a freshman
humanities course) and the assignment on which it is
based, and, in writing:
1.   Describe it according to the criteria (1-5) on
     the previous page that you applied to your
     own essay.
2.   Note mechanical and grammatical errors and
     describe them.
(If permissible, you may wish to mark the text and
make notes in the margin of the essay.)

Assignment: Choose two of the following: Isaiah,
Medieval Man, Plato, Leonardo, Sophocles, Galileo,
or Cicero. How would each respond if asked to describe the nature of the most important force in the
universe? (20%)

The world is full of seekers, inventors, artists

and philosophers. Each explaining their own views on

the nature of the world is made of, to get the people

to come to a clear understanding of *each of* their personal

thesis. But what may be said important by someone

may be meaningless to another. In this essay I will

explain the most important force of the universe seen

by Isaiah and Cicero. Isaiah, Where did the world

come from? Did it just form itself? Not to Isaiah.

Isaiah believed there was some ultimate being who

created people, heaven and earth. This person was

"God". "The creator of heaven and earth". "I have

made the earth, and created man upon it." "My hands

have stretched out the heavens and all their *host*

have I commanded. I have raised him up in righteous-

ness and I will direct all his ways. God created

Laws in which all humans are to accompany always. If

one wants to rest in heaven. God is one who punishes

9

and forgives, above all he guides all confused humans. (One relates to god in prayer and hopes for
his help). God wants all people to be fair. "God
does rule all men and ties all men to-gether were as
all men share the same god" God is the ultimate
reality he is the one we follow and gain our knowledge. To Isaiah there is NO other God. And that is
Isaiah's most important force of the universe.

Cicero, and his Laws which rules the whole universe by its wisdom in command and prohibition. He
distingushed what was considered to be righteous and
what was wrong. "For the divine mind cannot exist
without reason and the divine reason cannot but have
this power to establish right and wrong." Cicero believed the divine mind was the supreme Law, they were
invented for the safty of happiness of human life,
that those who first put statues of this kind in
force convinced their people that it was their intention to write down and put into effect such rules as
once accepted and adopted, *he tried to show people* ~~would make~~ it possible
for them *to live an* ~~and~~ honourable and happy life. Therefore
Law is the distinction between things just and unjust,
made an agreement with that the most ancient of all
things Nature: and in conformity to Nature's standard are framed those human laws which inflict punishment upon the wicked but defend and protect the
good.

10

In conclusion to each of these men and their contributions is that they all were great inventors and left to us great knowledge of how to study ~~art~~ the universe, to keep the laws in mind and to believe their is no other God but the God "creator of the heaven and earth. And these facts remain with us today.

Part Four: Roleplaying   Roleplay, with a fellow student, colleague, instructor, or program director, how you would transmit your evaluation of the above essay to its writer.

Part Five: Grammar Quiz   This quiz, which you will take yourself, may also be reproduced for use with your tutee when you begin your tutoring.

A. Pick out those sentences that contain run-ons or comma-splices and correct them:

    1. The leaves lay on the ground, we walked on them.
    2. You certainly were at the store. Mary saw you there.
    3. My two uncles drive trucks they are saving up to start their own business.
    4. Mr. Diaz is very friendly. He jokes with everyone.
    5. If your friends want to sleep over, they should bring sleeping bags.
    6. Carol stopped by last night she brought presents for the kids.
    7. That teacher was not fair he was not interested in the student's point of view.
    8. My camera broke consequently I have no pictures of my vacation.
    9. Doris came to the theater late therefore she missed the first act.
    10. Steve believed he was not speeding, however, this was far from the truth.

B. Correct those sentences that are not complete.

    1. Jogging by the quiet lake.
    2. Whenever Sheila plays her records.
    3. Pushed into a corner and shaking with fear.
    4. Before he joined the army.
    5. When she cries, I feel sad.
    6. Since he began studying Latin in the college on Tuesday evenings.

7. He never wanted to join the club. Although we all made it clear that we liked him and wanted him to.
8. If we can just suffer with it a few more weeks.
9. There will be lots of food for everyone.
10. Sandra put on her new hat.

C. Correct the following sentences:

1. Between you and I, we should be able to carry the boxes from the car to the garage.
2. I like the group of which I'm part of alot.
3. John told me I am coming to the film showing tonight.
4. The person that gave me the lead on the hospital scandal asked to remain anonymous.
5. Swimming an average of twenty-five laps daily, the pool is used by staff members as well as by the students.
6. One idea proposed to compensate for layoffs is that each worker would be responsible for cleaning up their own work area.
7. Hidden by the wall cars enter traffic without any warning to oncoming vehicles.
8. The workers uniforms and shoes as well as specialized equipment, such as goggles, are the companies.
9. The students status remained in doubt.
10. The work for her and I is easy.

D. Pick the correct word from parentheses and write it in the blank.

1. Here (is, are)_____the courses we are taking in college.
2. Lawrence, as well as his sister, (want, wants)_____to buy the property.
3. Over the hills (sit, sits)_____our family home.
4. The hat with all the bells (is, are)_____ the one I want.
5. There (was, were)_____several patients waiting for the doctor.

12

Tutee Profile

Once you have ascertained your own strengths and weaknesses, you are ready to begin tutoring. In the tutoring profile you do most preliminary evaluation and planning with your tutee. Assessment is a shared process during which both of you use your knowledge and experience about writing to make a tutoring plan.

Can You Work With This Person?* As we discussed in The Tutor Book some persons are not best served by the tutorial: they might need preliminary work to prepare them for working with a tutor, or they may have problems beyond the scope of the writing tutorial. Since it is possible your tutee may be in one of these categories, you and your tutee should examine the following questions before you talk about writing:

1. Can the person see well enough to read printed material on paper or on the blackboard? Sight problems can greatly handicap the person's ability to write and edit.

2. Does the person hear well enough to follow lecture, classroom discussion, and ordinary conversation? Hearing problems can interfere with the person's understanding of class and tutorial material. If you suspect hearing or sight problems, discuss with your tutee the feasibility of his or her getting tested. Hearing aids and/or glasses can change a person's whole attitude toward learning.

3. Can the student read and understand class assignments and tests? Reading problems can interfere with a person's ability to understand what an answer or essay requires. If you suspect a negative answer to this question, talk to the student about seeing a reading counselor or working with a reading tutor at the same time he or she is working with you. (See also the reading and study skills tutoring pamphlet in this series.)

---

* Many of these categories were compiled by Larry Klein in "Techniques for Tutors," an unpublished paper given at a Special Session on Writing Centers, Annual Conference of the National Council of Teachers of English, November, 1977.

4. Can the person follow what you are saying and, if necessary, act upon it? Personal or physiological problems may distract the student, and nervousness may interfere with comprehension. In either case, you should recommend the person see a counselor who can best diagnose the problems. A reading counselor will probably be able to provide services or direct your tutee to appropriate agencies.

5. Can the person complete relatively long and complex sentences? Psychological or learning disabilities can interfere with the writing process in its most simple phases. It might be necessary for the person to receive some appropriate therapy before he or she can attempt to write complex essays.

Some of these problems will not surface until you have worked with the student for a period of time. Therefore, you should refer to this list during the course of your tutoring. When and if you make suggestions to your tutee about other sources of help, you should do so tactfully and judiciously. Remember, referrals are not ways to avoid working with difficult students.

Writing Inventory Most tutees can be helped within the tutorial relationship, however, and a good way you and your tutee can decide what form the tutorial should take is by examining the tutee's approaches to writing. Such a discussion has the advantage of getting the person to talk about writing in a positive way, emphasizing what he or she does rather than the mistakes he or she has made. Also, it demands the person's active involvement. The person is doing most of the talking and is talking about writing in a serious and systematic way. This task may be written.

Writing History You and your tutee should explore what kinds of writing the tutee has done in the past. Go as far back as possible in the student's academic career and outline the writing courses taken, what these courses required in length and quality of the required writing, what formal writing concepts (e.g., grammar, outlining) these courses included, how writing was evaluated, and how the student performed according to the evaluation criteria established.

You should also question tutees about their non-classroom writing experience. Do they write to family and friends? Are they responsible for correspondence and memos, or for completing lab or other technical reports at work? Have they done any writing as part of their responsibilities in church, lodge, or

14

other community organizations? Some students may have mastered writing through informal learning at home or on the job and need to be shown how some academic writing is similar to or differs from what they already know and how they can build on it. Conversely, the kinds of writing your tutees are responsible for at work or home may help you focus your tutoring on relevant material. Also, knowing when, if, and under what circumstances your tutees have learned their material will help you shape your tutoring strategies.

Attitudes about Writing   Along with exploring what kinds of writing the tutee has done in the past, you two should also be discussing how the student felt about writing--in grammar and high school and in any other situations in which writing was required. Ascertaining the person's attitudes may be somewhat difficult. Probably the person hasn't analyzed these feelings beyond the common, "I hate to write" or "I have nothing to say" feeling (or the less common, "I kind of like it" or "It's fun"). Therefore, you may have to translate abstract attitudes into specific examples such as, "What kind of assignment do you like, dislike?" "How do you feel about beginning a paper?" "How do you respond to deadlines?" "How do you feel about writing in class?" "What part of the writing process do you like best? Least?" "What have been your most and least successful classroom or other formal writing experiences and why?" Start with a list of questions but try to get the conversation to flow easily and offer the person a way to air feelings --positive and negative.

Writing Habits   At this time you should also be discussing with tutees how they go about writing. As habit is, by nature, automatic, persons may (as with attitudes) have some difficulty picking out exactly how they write; therefore, a list of questions can be helpful to start an illuminating discussion. Such matters as how far in advance the person begins to write after being given an assignment, how much time the writer devotes to research, the first draft, the second draft, tables and graphs, editing, and proofreading can offer very helpful information. Does the writer dictate, write papers out by hand, or type? How does the writer make corrections on the final draft? Where does the person write: in the office or at a desk at home, in a quiet dorm or bedroom, at the library, in front of the TV or with the stereo blaring? With a friend or alone? When does the person write: at night, during lunch break, on weekends, or after class?

Relationship with Teacher, Supervisor or Readers/
Knowledge of Requirements   Since most college students write for teachers, the tutee's relationship
with the teacher is crucial to his or her successfully completing a writing assignment. As a tutor,
you need to know how well the tutee understands what
the teacher wants on home assignments and in-class
essay exams; does the student understand such things
as how long a paper must be, in what form it should
be handed in (and when), how much outside research is
necessary, and whether footnotes and bibliography are
required? And if so, does the student know what style
manual he or she must follow? Does the student know
how much the paper or exam will count towards the
final grade? Can the student understand the teacher's
grading symbols and paper comments--and what use to
make of them? Are rewrites necessary? Permissible?
Most important, does the student feel the teacher is
approachable if there are misunderstandings or con-
flicts about grades, etc.?
     Writers in business and industry must also be
aware of similar constraints. Is the writing intended
for a single individual, a group of insiders, external
use? Does the writer understand the assignment and
the scope? (What is the report to cover?) What form
is it to follow? (Is there a house manual which dic-
tates these matters?) How long is it to be? Will
other persons be writing additional sections? Will
there be a review process and an opportunity for revision? Will others be responsible for final editing
or must the writer assume this responsibility?

Composing: Process and Revision   Finally, in order
to assess the person's needs, you will need to find
out how the person actually writes a paper. As we
have suggested, this will probably be the most difficult part of the inventory since most writers, especially if they are beginners, do not think about
their writing process because they are so anxious
about their product. Some general questions, listed
below, should help get the conversation going; however, your best technique may be to watch your tutee
write something from start to finish (perhaps while
you write along), and then to discuss the process.
What you will be looking for (and these are questions
you can ask your tutee before he or she begins writing) is:

     Before Writing   What are the person's pre-writing
strategies; that is, how does the tutee come up with
the topic and ideas on developing the topic?
     How does the person gather ideas to develop the
topic?
     Does the person think about the aim of the essay,

the audience to whom it is addressed, and his or her relationship to that audience (tone) before developing the paper?

During Writing How does the person decide on the organizational pattern of the paper?
How does the person turn his/her notes into actual written discussion?

Revision How does the person check for coherence, unity, development?
How does the person check for elements that clearly reflect the organizational pattern he or she has chosen?
How does the person check for syntactical elements to ensure clarity, transition, sentence variety?
How does the person check for correct and appropriate language, especially language that helps define and reach the audience for whom the paper is written?

Proofreading How does the person check for mechanical elements such as punctuation, tense, verb form, spelling?

III. THE TUTEE PLAN: THE WRITING CONTRACT

The inventory, if done thoroughly, will yield a lot of valuable information and should tell you in what areas the writer needs help. Nonetheless, you will have to start planning long before you've developed a complete or total picture, probably by the end of the first session or at least by the second. As we discussed in Chapter 2 of <u>The</u> <u>Tutor</u> <u>Book</u>, the writing contract offers you a good structure within which to make your plan, whether it is a formal document or an informal guide. Feel free to use the guide on page 19 or create your own. Once you have made the contract, it should be subject to frequent assessment.

Short-term Goals

Short-term goals concern those urgent matters that need to be handled before anything else is done. Your tutee may have gotten back a paper that has to be revised in two weeks;* he or she may have a writing assignment due in one week--or less. Your short-term goals will be to help your tutee with these assignments.

Other short-term goals might develop from what you find out in your analysis of the person's writing habits. If the person isn't planning his or her time efficiently or is working in noisy or distracting conditions, your short-term, or preliminary, goals may center on ways to help the person improve his or her writing habits.

---

*If your student does not bring you a graded paper, ask for a writing sample, since all assessment is contingent on your familiarity with the student's writing.

Learning Contract

Name_____Term_____Year_____

Course_____

Teacher_____

Tutor_____

Learning Goal(s):

    Short-term

    Long-term

Tasks (in priority order)	Deadlines	Comments

Long-term Goals

Long-term goals concern the tutoring work you and your tutee will be doing all term or longer. They should evolve from general problems your tutee has been having with his or her writing. The profile, sample writing, and the writing inventory, should be the basis for developing these goals. You might discover, for example, that your tutee can easily find and develop ideas but has no method for proofreading; in that case, proofreading will be the place to begin. Another writer may have trouble getting started. Once she has her topic, she is fine. Another writer's problems may be in the syntactic realm: his writing is often incoherent, clumsy, and awkward. Long-term goals may also involve increasing self-confidence, lessening writing anxiety, and developing other objectives related to attitudes. Most frequently, the inventory will show that the writer needs work in more than one area and you will need to develop a range of tasks to achieve one or more goals.

Tasks

Once you and your tutee have decided on feasible goals for the term (or session) you will need to make your plans concrete and to set priorities. Tasks are specific activities which will help you accomplish your goals.

A good method of finding appropriate tasks is to brainstorm with your tutee, starting with the short-term goals. For example, if your tutee's short-term goal is to complete a social science paper due next week, ask her what she thinks needs to be done in order to write her paper. She may already have her topic, an analysis of ERA's failure in New York State, but she still needs a thesis. First, she needs to do some reading, thinking, listing, grouping. Then she can go on to develop a thesis, organize, and write. Her tasks, listed in logical order, might read: reading, thinking, listing, grouping, developing a thesis, organizing, writing, and if there is time, revising the paper.

Her long-term goals, however, go beyond this paper. One area she is generally unhappy with is her spelling. No matter how well she writes, bad spelling gets in the way. Again, brainstorm with her. Your query about past mistakes may help her realize she can learn from her mistakes, and she decides to retrieve past papers, make a list of errors, and put each, spelled correctly, in a sentence. You know of a good film strip on spelling, and a collection of exercises the center happens to own. Add those to the list of tasks. Can you teach her some rules? she asks. Well, you don't know them too well, but you can certainly learn them in time for that session. Your list would look like this: list of student's errors, words spelled correctly in sentences, rules, filmstrip, exercises, practice writing. Her own errors would be addressed because they are immediately relevant; rules will provide a context for correct spelling in the future; filmstrips and exercises can reinforce her new knowledge, and practice writing can help her see whether she has improved.

Deadlines

Try to put a deadline next to each task, a date by which your tutee completes the task. This will give your sessions a clear direction, something to aim for. Of course, things come up and people learn at different rates, so these deadlines should not be rigid; rather they should give you and the tutee a sense of what needs to be done and when.

Practice Activity

Assessment is one of the most difficult tutoring skills for a new tutor to master, yet essential in setting priorities and determining your plan. For this reason, we include a sample paper and assignment with which to develop this skill, and ask you to write a contract based on this material. You might want to share this contract with your supervisor or a senior tutor.

The assignment for the following paper called for an expository and analytic essay defining "community" and its characteristic features. The student presents this sample as a rough draft. Your contract should have several parts: short- and long-term goals, tasks in order of priority; and, finally, deadlines by when these tasks should be accomplished. (Of course, you are making the contract solely on the basis of a writing sample; in actuality, you will be determining the contractual goals based on your meeting a person, and the general profile you will develop.)

The three ~~symbolic~~ street dividng stripes, symbolically colored in red, white & green, descend from steep incline providing a "yellow brick road" like pathway into Federal Hill

As one ascends, ~~the~~ uneaven, coarse cobblestones, their cracks filled with dirt, ~~scraps~~ shreds of tatered paper, ~~old stale~~ hardened chewing gum and lose granite make the journey difficult. The narrow streets are cluttered by a consitant wall

united series of shops. Each ~~shop~~ providing a territory ~~hang out~~ claimed by one of the many groups that can be located nightly on the corners. ~~in the winter~~ Upon enterning a shop, whether it be a dog grooming salon, a bakery, a small market ot the local barber, one is surround immediately by the barrage of deep husky manlike Italian voices. Hands can be seen flying freely through the air, their motions accompanying the words spoken. There is one man & one shop which represents the whole community perfectly. He ~~walks around~~ staggers, revealing ~~his age, he , his his powder white hair rests firmly~~ Upon entrance, the aroma arouses ones hunger. The smell of rich, deli-cheese ~~smells~~ along with thick zesty sauce and

22

warm home-baked bread ~~can almost be tasted~~ causes ones mouth to water. The old Italian man saying "Comeona in" Hav'

a taste its a good." can be seen with extended arms

in the center of the grain covered dull gray cement

floor. He poses there, his apron covered with

sauces, ~~crumbs~~ smudges of raw fresh meants and evi-

dence of whatever else he prepared that day. His

smile, warm & glowing invites the brouser into his

home and makes one less weary about accepting the

offered taste. He is surrounded by long glass cases

which home his Italian feast. Behind the counters

there are several heavy-set, dark haired Italian

women rolling their hands in dough, stirring the

~~coldrin coldrin~~ vats of gravy and making other prepara-

tions. The walls are covered by yellowed, unframed ~~pictures~~

family & scenic pictures from the Old Country. Beams

crossing the ceiling are decorated by hanging sala-

mies, logs of ropetied cheeses and ~~bottles of wine in~~

~~a~~ straw baskets containg bottles of wine. The archi-

tecture of the building promotes the Little Italy

feeling. The windows are of a half circular shape.

The front wall is constructed from old brick with as

many cracks as the cobble stone. The shops decore is

completed by a paint chipped, wood split signs which

reads "Providence Cheese." From here on, both shops

& people continue to appear the same.

IV. THE COMPOSING PROCESS

Helping someone compose can be as frustrating as it is rewarding. You, as tutor, have skills your tutee does not. Ways of sharpening the thesis, organizing and developing the essay, and ways of proofreading it may seem obvious to you. You will be tempted to take the pen and write the essay yourself or, at least, to <u>tell</u> the student what to do. As we have mentioned many times in <u>The Tutor Book</u> (and earlier in this one), doing and telling students how to write or writing for them will not help them improve in any permanent way. It will not even make them feel better, because they will know that they didn't really write the essay. Your job is to guide them to methods that will help them generate their own ideas and put these into writing. In the sections below a compendium of methods will help writers master various aspects of the writing process. You will probably find it helpful to try these methods yourself before offering them to your tutee.

Pre-writing

When we refer to pre-writing we refer to all that a writer can do to loosen up and get ideas flowing, to find a topic to write about (when that is not a given), and to develop ideas about that topic before beginning to write.

<u>Free Writing</u> is based on the free association of ideas that goes on continually in our minds. When we are thinking randomly and without any apparent purpose, we are free associating. One popular way to free write is to write continuously, without stopping, for 10 minutes (or anywhere from 10 to 25 minutes)-- about anything that enters your mind. The trick is that you cannot correct and you cannot stop. If you have nothing to say you must write just that, or scream on paper at whomever is asking you to do this exercise. Not only is free writing a good way to "ventilate," but it can also be fun. And it does make people more comfortable with writing and less afraid of the blank page by encouraging ideas to flow. Free

writing regularly, by the way, can have an important
cumulative effect in making writing easier and more
pleasant.

The Writer's Journal is a variation of the journal
we described in Chapter 1 of The Tutor Book. Like
the traditional journal, it is a place to record
facts and feelings; but it also provides a resource
for the writer to develop writing skill. Jackie
Goldsby's Journal is a good example. (See Bibliography.) In journals, writers can jot down ideas for
writing, incidents, characterizations, descriptions,
rationales. They can practice techniques, such as
dialogue, mood building, humor. For beginning writers, the journal is an arena in which they can write
and not be judged, where they can write just for the
fun of it or write to practice skills they feel they
need. The journal is also a place where tutees can
practice pre-writing techniques on their own. Encourage your tutees to keep journals. Show them examples
of other writers' journals, even your own. Ask to
see your tutees' journals every so often to encourage
them to keep up with it. (After a while they won't
need this "encouragement.") Be careful, however, not
to evaluate the journal, except to point out areas in
which the student has been particularly creative.

Meditation is a technique based on methods commonly
used in religion or philosophy to bring the meditant
in touch with spiritual matters or serious concerns.
It is a way of clearing the mind of distractions and
of concentrating on one idea. For this reason, it
can be an excellent means of helping writers to think
out what they want to say, and to help them lessen
their anxiety, remove distractions, and concentrate
deeply on what they are doing. If you are working
in a noisy, crowded room, try to move your student to
a quiet, undistracting environment: an empty office
or classroom, dorm room, or a grassy area. Then
leave him or her alone for a specified period of time
(20-30 minutes). When you come back you can discuss
what the student learned or ask her/him to write it
down. If moving to a quiet area is impossible, try
to create a calm environment where you are by using
a cubicle, a "do not disturb" sign, perhaps even
chanting with your student softly (e.g., "om" in different keys) and concentrating on breathing (5 seconds
in to 10 seconds out).

Physical Activity As unlikely as meditation and
exercise as spurs to writing may seem, these are both
valid and important ways to get one ready to write.
Vigorous, solitary physical activity, like running and
swimming, can clear the mind and release ideas.

25

Invention

One could call free writing a form of invention and, indeed, invention is often classed under pre-writing; however, in this pamphlet, when we refer to invention we will be talking about methods specifically designed to help people discover what they have to say about a given subject. In some composition texts invention methods are called heuristics or problem-solving strategies.

Acting-a-Story; Acting Out a Scenario   In Chapter 4 of The Tutor Book we discussed how simulation-games help people to practice necessary problem-solving techniques. Acting-a-story, a form of simulation gaming, is an especially effective heuristic, for it gives writers the opportunity to make real decisions within a realistic environment and, in doing this, to think topics through thoroughly. The ideas they develop through acting-a-story can then be transferred to their writing, which should be more clearly and logically reasoned as a result of such roleplaying.
    Some simulation-games have been specially developed to structure writing situations and are commercially available (see Troyka and Nudelman's Taking Action in the bibliography). However, you can devise your own scenarios by getting your writers to role-play situations relevant to their writing assignment. For example, if your writer has to reply to a letter of complaint, have him or her act out the role of the irate customer--you can play the sales manager. If the writer has to develop advertising copy, have her "sell" you on the product or service. Or, if the writer has to write about Pride and Prejudice, have him argue his interpretation of the novel with you. You will find the writer's involvement will be high because drama is involving. And forced to think about and resolve immediate problems, he or she will discover the many sides to each situation.

The 5 Ws and an H   Reporters have long used the 5 Ws and an H--who, what, where, when, why, and how--to make sure they have covered all they need to about a subject quickly and thoroughly. In answering the six questions as they pertain to a particular subject (e.g., report of a conference or meeting), the writer will have a structure within which to develop ideas.

26

1. Where did I go?
2. When did it begin, end?
3. Whom did I go with and whom did I meet?
4. Why did I go?
5. What did I do?
6. And how did it turn out?

Brainstorming   Brainstorming is not new to people in business where it is often used by a group to solve problems and generate ideas. Adapted to writing, brainstorming allows individuals to stimulate each other to develop material for written projects. The ideas can then be grouped into categories and, if possible, a thesis can be found from what is gathered.

Brainstorming resembles free writing in that it calls for free association; however, it differs from it in ultimately appealing to the more conscious and rational parts of the mind. Also, it is usually done orally because of its group nature. The process may be adapted to individual tutoring like this:

- Get a large piece of paper or use a blackboard.
- Ask the writer to call out all his or her ideas on a given subject and write these down, no matter whether or not they pertain to the subject and whether or not they make sense.
- See if the student can find groupings under which to list a number of similar ideas. (At this point you may want to eliminate some ideas that don't fit under any grouping.)
  One of these groupings can ultimately become the basis for a thesis. Or encourage your tutee to find a thesis that connects all the ideas.

Questioning   Tutors can use questioning techniques to help tutees develop their ideas. One such technique sees the topic in terms of a question or series of questions. For example, your tutee's topic may be Italian Renaissance painting. What questions can be made from that subject? Which were the key painters and why? Why was Leonardo Da Vinci so important? Why is the Mona Lisa still considered one of the best of the Renaissance paintings? (Notice the questions get narrower and more focussed so that the answer to the last question can, once the process is completed, serve as the thesis of a paper.)

You may also be interested in using the formal questioning techniques of Aristotle's Topoi or Pike's Wave Theory.

Aristotelian Categories   Aristotle (384-322 B.C.), the great Greek philosopher, first developed the following categories or classifications (topoi, from which our modern word topics derives) as aids to orators. He believed that these topoi were universal,

27

that is, they could be used to develop any subject at all. (To know them was the mark of an Athenian educated to fulfill his obligations as a citizen.)

Definition: What is it? What group does it belong to?

Comparison: How is it similar to or different from things in its grouping?

Relationship: What causes bring it about and what effect does it have (or can it have)? What came before it? What are the difficulties about having it?

Circumstances: What can and cannot happen to it or because of it?

Testimony: What have famous or eminent figures said about it? What statistics are available on it? What rules or laws exist about it?

<u>Tagmemics</u>   This is a problem-solving strategy based on linguistics and physics. It is a way of finding out the answers to any conceivable question. As interpreted by Young, Becker, and Pike in <u>Rhetoric: Discovery and Change</u>, questions about a topic can be explored by analyzing its contrastive features, its range of variation, and, finally, its distribution. The contrastive features are those features unique to the thing (or idea) in question (in contrast to anything else). The range of variation refers to how much the item can vary and still remain itself. Distribution refers to the context of the item, where it occurs in space and time.

Suppose the topic of a paper were appropriate student behavior in a college classroom. First, defining the topic as a <u>particle</u>, we would want to find the unique features of student behavior (as opposed to teacher behavior, high school student behavior, etc.). Then we would define student behavior as a <u>wave</u> and explore the variations in acceptable behavior. How much and in what ways can students "vary" from fellow students and still be acceptable. Finally, we would want to know when and where people take on student behavior. This involves examining student behavior in the context of a <u>field</u>, or within a system. When does the context make student behavior unacceptable?, for example.

Such an analysis, when done thoroughly, can offer a full understanding of a topic.

<u>Talking it Through</u>   Sometimes talking can be a less painful way of discovering ideas and developing details than writing and thus offers a good prelude to the actual writing of an essay. Once the writer has

28

some idea of what he or she wants to write about, ask the writer to tell you about it--to talk it through. (Tutor: "What are you going to say next? And after that? Tell me about the railway station. Is it indoors or outside? How many people work at the station? Describe some of the workers. How many trains were there? What colors were they?) By probing for details you get your tutee to think about details. Likewise, by asking for connections, you get the writer to think about transitions. You can easily see how the invention technique of talking a "paper" can emerge from the pre-writing activity of acting a story.

Looping is a variation of free writing that allows one to free write on a particular subject. It may evolve as you form associations and what begins as formless writing becomes centered around a specific topic. Or you may choose to loop on an assigned topic, especially when you are not quite sure whether or not you have anything to say or are not sure what you want to say. In one version, developed by Peter Elbow in Writing Without Teachers and by Cowan and Cowan in Writing, you can do the following: write freely on a given topic but without working at staying focussed on that topic. (If you go off it, in other words, that's okay). Then draw a line and summarize the gist of that loop or locate its "center of gravity" (which may or may not be the idea you started out with). Use the "gist" or "center of gravity" sentence as the topic sentence of the next loop. The point here is to discover and then develop an idea that gets you interested and starts your writing "cooking," so that a paper gradually emerges from the looping process.

Let's say your topic is 19th-century trade agreements: in your free writing, you record names and dates and explore how boring this topic is because it's not about people; so your "center of gravity" sentence might be "Trade agreements don't have anything to do with people." Immediately after you begin writing again, you think of the slave trade and how it must have felt for people to be treated as commodities and cargo. You've found your topic!

In another version, discussed by Peter Elbow in Writing With Power, you use looping if you've already done some planning and thinking, when you've read some slave trade agreements and interpretations of them, for example. In this case, Elbow suggests writing down all your responses, first thoughts, hunches, prejudices, and assumptions. Later in this process, you might write dialogues (between a slave and her buyer? between a Wall Street banker and the slave trader?),

stories, or even freeze-frame actions, and vary your
audience and voice (either writing to, or as if you
were, a free black man in the early 19th century; a
feminist in the late 20th). Even if something doesn't
seem to relate directly (an image of Rousseau's
Sleeping Gypsy), it may help to point to a connection
you're making. Thus looping consists of two parts:
the voyage out and the voyage in--a loop. The voyage
out lets your imagination rove. On the voyage back,
you look at what you've got and what you can do with
it. This will lead to actual composing.

Aim, Audience, Voice

In the Art of Rhetoric, Aristotle addressed him-
self to those people who most frequently needed to
develop an argument: the political orator, the legis-
lator, those in the legal profession. As the Aristotelian tradition developed, rhetoric was extended to
mean writing persuasively. While Aristotle was concerned with helping orators and "lawyers" understand
the nature of proper reasoning, he emphasized that arguments were effective only if the speakers considered
the aim or purpose of the argument, the audience the
speaker was seeking to persuade, and finally, the im-
pression the speaker wished to give. Modern educators
interested in understanding more about writing have
returned to Aristotle and found a source of strategies which might be useful to beginning writers.

Aim   James Kinneavy, in his comprehensive work, A
Theory of Discourse, separates the aims of written
discourse into four areas: referential, expressive,
argumentative, and literary. Referential, or technical, writing covers all writing that refers to something else, for example, scientific writing, which
refers to laws or experiments, or informational writing which refers to facts and events. Argumentative
writing is writing whose aim is persuasion, while the
purpose of expressive writing is to express an idea
or feeling, and the main "point" of literary writing
is to give ideas aesthetic shape and form. Your tutees should be encouraged to consider the aim of their
discourse, as it is intimately related to the way
their ideas are expressed.
    Suppose your student has chosen the topic of
birthdays. A literary paper might be a poem or short
story centering on a birthday celebration. An

expressive paper might use some of the <u>literary</u> devices, of description, dialogue, or narrative, but its chief aim, to which these devices are subordinate, is to <u>explain</u> the writer's experience, feelings, and ideas about celebrating birthdays. An argumentative paper might have as its aim convincing the reader that birthday celebrations should be dispensed with; again you might show the tutee that a dramatic example of a disastrous birthday party and the discussion of the personal trauma the writer suffered might be used to support such an argument but without other reasons and discussion the paper might not prove sufficiently convincing. Finally, the student, assigned a referential or research paper, might consider exploring birthdays from a historical point of view (e.g., the development of birthday celebrations in France and Italy), sociologically (birthdays as a ritual function of class, race, or community), or in literature (why there is no birthday party in <u>Who's Afraid of Virginia Woolf</u>?). (Of course the student who has done research on birthdays can use this material as well to bolster an argument, to give greater expressive power to an essay, or to shape a literary work.) Thus knowing the aim of an essay can help a student understand how to subordinate knowledge and content to a particular end or purpose.

You will find, however, that writers do not typically think about aim or that their thinking does not go beyond "I have to do it because my instructor (or supervisor) assigned it." Often this attitude is justified either because the topic assigned suggests one purpose or another, or because the topic has been so defined as purposely to restrict the writer's aim. An example of the former might be "The Action of Plastics at Temperatures Beyond the Boiling Point" (clearly scientific or technical in nature); an example of the latter is an essay in which the writer is asked to take a position for or against federalism (clearly argumentative writing). Since similar writing is often required on tests and at work, you should make the writer aware that many writing courses are devoted to teaching the skills necessary for such academic work, and ultimately for a given profession and, therefore, professors shape assignments to take the aims of other disciplines into account. (The examples above might pertain, respectively, to chemistry or a technical course on synthetics and to a political science or history course.)

Practice Activity

1. Using each of the following topics, have the writer define a particular aim and briefly sketch one

or more strategies for developing an essay in accordance with it: social classes, July 4, minority rights, the automobile, lanterns.

2. Have your tutee consider the following topics and how they might be affected by the writer's aims:

    a.   honest political candidate
        1. campaign literature
        2. discussion of candidate's record for a political weekly
        3. response to a political slander in the local newspaper

    b. work
        1. an essay intended to amuse
        2. a detailed job description (for a prospective employer)
        3. a volunteer-recruitment effort

Audience   In many writing courses, the teacher is a model of the educated or informed audience--the ideal reader to whom a paper is addressed. Yet writing teachers are so concerned with having their students "prove" themselves as writers that instructors may demand, much to the students' bewilderment, continual explanation and clarification of statements and arguments which the student presumes the teacher already knows. Likewise a supervisor may make similar demands. Often writers react to these demands by explaining even the most obvious points (sometimes to be told that their readers aren't stupid). This problem is compounded by two factors: one is that writers are frequently unaware that they are not being clear or coherent. Second, the novice writer often does not yet know what knowledge is "common" knowledge. Writers cannot therefore predict what may be either obvious or insulting to the "ideal" or well-informed reader. What students of writing need to learn, however, is not how to write for an ideal audience but for a specific audience. As they specialize in college they will have to write for a specific academic discipline; later, if they become employed within this discipline, they must learn to write for their colleagues, who are specialists in their fields. Only after an extensive review process will a report, advertising copy, or product descriptions be considered final and ready to be duplicated, bound, and distributed.
    The best way, then, for writers to get a general sense of audience is for them to work with their peers, reading each other's papers and evaluating them

along with the teacher or supervisor. This will be discussed at greater length under Peer Critiques. You, the tutor, represent still another version of audience and are in the best position to give students immediate feedback on what is clear and not clear. Also, you can help your writer develop a sense of audience by "playing" different audiences: college newspaper editor, science professor, consumer, manufacturer, etc.

<u>Practice Activity</u>

1. Suppose you were writing on changes in American immigration laws during the past fifty years. Fill in Column 3 with some of the material you will need to include in your essay for each aim and audience. The first one has been done for you.

Aim	Audience	Material
Referential	American Teen-ager	What are the laws now? How have they changed? What were the practical results of their changing? Who was most affected by the laws?
a. Expressive	New Immigrant	
b. Argumenta-tive	Conservative Organization	
c. Referential	Liberal Magazine	

2. Have your student mold three essays out of the following topics and audience (if related to your student's courses) and discuss how the material and style of an assignment growing out of each pairing would differ according to the selected audience.

Topic	Audience
a. conference/convention	1. prospective participants (scholars)
	2. prospective participants (salespeople for the company)
	3. hotel staff
b. new drug	1. buyers (consumers)
	2. doctors
	3. Federal Drug Administration
c. movie	1. newspaper reader
	2. fellow movie buffs
	3. literary critics
d. Mt. Ida	1. travel section readers
	2. classicists
	3. geologists/earth Science students
e. modern dance company	1. Phys Ed. student
	2. aesthetics class
	3. historians

Suppose, for instance, your tutee, who is a Business Management major, was asked to write on the annual convention of office machines held at the local hotel. Your student decides to write a report on the convention for the sales manager of his or her fictitious company. The material included in this report will have to be accurate, related to company interests, specific and to the point, offering suggestions for how the company can use what the employee learned at the convention. The style must be formal, in that it is an official report to a superior officer, and objective, so that the employer will take the report seriously as being without bias, and, thus, useful to the company.

Voice   You will find aim, audience, and voice are related. Of all these, voice is the most complex—and the most difficult to discern. In the most obvious and simple cases, if the writer is addressing a

friendly audience that agrees with him or her, the
voice will be warm and friendly. If the writer's aim
is to inform a knowledgeable reader about a subject,
the voice will be crisp and professional; if the writer is expressing a feeling to a close friend (in a
love letter, perhaps), the voice will be familiar and
intimate. Voice is also dictated by the writer's relationship to his or her material. Writers may be
humorous about the activities they describe; or they
may commit themselves to writing totally from
"within." Technical writing, on the other hand, often
requires an objective stance and one which places a
high value on the speaker's precision and accuracy.
    Here, for example, is one sort of description--of
a whaling ship--that seems subjective:

> She was apparelled like any barbaric Ethiopian
> emperor, his neck heavy with pendants of polished
> ivory. She was a thing of trophies. A cannibal
> of craft, tricking herself forth in the chased
> bones of her enemies. All round, her unpanelled,
> open bulwarks were garnished like one continuous
> jaw, with the sharp teeth of the sperm whale, in-
> serted there for pins, to fasten her old hempen
> thews and tendons to.... Scorning a turnstile
> wheel at her reverend helm, she sported there a
> tiller; and that tiller was in one mass, curiously
> carved of her hereditary foe....A noble craft, but
> somehow a most melancholy!

This is the voice of one well-traveled in the wide
world and in the world of literature. It is a voice
tinged at once with epic mockery and awe. The boat is
grotesque and ferocious both conveying an admiration
and an intimate identification with the boat and its
grandeur. In his assessment of the boat, we learn as
much about the writer as we do about the ship: there
can be no doubt that this is a sailor speaking. Despite its load of metaphor and simile, the voice is
careful (in its description) and knowledgeable about
boats in general and, therefore, of this boat's
archaic features.
    If we turn to another excerpt, the voice is no-
ticeably different:

> One of the most interesting things about six-
> teenth- and seventeenth-century ships is how they
> were steered. The steering wheel, which seems to
> us such an obvious contrivance, had not yet been
> invented, and the tiller was controlled by means
> of a device called in English the 'whipstaff'....
> The diagram in Fig. 103 is intended to show how
> the whipstaff worked.... When it blew hard the

whipstaff had to be disconnected altogether, and
steering had to be done by means of tackles on
the tiller. It was an unsatisfactory contrivance
in many ways, and the wheel, when it appeared,
must have been a real boon.

Both passages are about ships (and in particular
about the steering mechanism), and give very specific
details. The two are equally steeped in experience
and historical knowledge and we can "see" clearly what
is being described. Yet the second writer feels that
only a diagram will be effective in explaining the dy-
namic forces at work, while the first never gives up
on words. Both writers offer a direct personal reve-
lation of point of view (or opinion): yet subject
matter and feeling, experience and history are not so
immediately fused in the second passage as in the
first. We do not feel the lure of the sea with quite
the same fervor, either, because even as the latter
writer takes us into the past, he also distances us
by reminding us of the technological rewards of progress. If sympathetic to the sailor of old, he is
grateful to be living in the modern world.
    Problems with voice are among the most awkward in
writing because they are so linked to the sense of
sound or tone. If the voice is inappropriate we
"hear" it before we see it in words. For example, a
love letter written with a scholarly voice hardly con-
veys love, despite apparent sentiment. A job application letter written in a warm, intimate voice mars
the intention to convey professionalism and respect.
A good way to familiarize your tutees with voice is to
give them parallel writing passages from a variety of
materials (such as those used in the above example)
and ask them to identify the voice, picking out words
and phrases that identify tone. You might write your
own as well as choose from student writing and published works. *

Practice Activity

    First, identify the voice of the following para-
graphs, picking out words and phrases that generate
tone, then rewrite each passage using a new voice.

---

    * The quotations above were, respectively, from
Melville's Moby-Dick, or The Whale (1851) and Romola
and R.C. Anderson's The Sailing Ship: Six Thousand
Years of History (New York: Bonanza Books, 1963),
pp. 155, 156, 157. Notice that the dual authorship
of the latter does not negate the idea of a single
voice created in the writing.

1. To: Math Lab Tutors
    From: L. Awnet
    Re: Tidiness

    I hardly thought I'd have to be writing you
    about this subject; after all, the math lab is
    a "home" to most of you for ten or more hours a
    week. It is, therefore, inconceivable to me that
    you could leave the tutor lounge as filthy as you
    have been during this term. Cigarette butts lie
    all over the floor, squashed soda cans litter the
    tables, the couch has a number of cigarette holes,
    and, worse still, unfinished food is left every-
    where.
    It is not surprising that mice have been
    spotted; now the custodian has threatened to de-
    clare the place a health hazard and lock us all
    out. Thus, I am left with no choice but to put
    you all on warning. <u>If the staff lounge is not</u>
    <u>noticeably cleaner in two weeks, it will be closed</u>
    <u>for the year</u>.

2. When one thinks of Italian wines, one usually
    thinks of chianti. If one knows something of
    Italy, one might have heard of Soave, Valpoli-
    cella, or maybe even Barolo. However, the true
    <u>vinaio</u> (that means wine drinker, in Italian) knows
    that the diamond of Italian wines comes from the
    Sienese hills, <u>le colle senese</u>, where Brunello di
    Montalcino is made.

3. Cerena Scott is not an elegant writer; no, ele-
    gance hardly matters where her writing is con-
    cerned; precisely because she is aiming beyond
    elegance, her style might, in fact, be called
    supra-elegant. It transcends elegance. Indeed,
    it transcends any definitions this humble critic
    may advance.

4. Look, this is a hard thing for me to write. I've
    been working here four years, and you and Gus have
    been terrific to me. You've really taught me all
    I know about car repair, and a little more that I
    was too thick to learn. Well, now it's time for
    me to leave. I got a really good job over at
    Elite Electronics, and they promised I'd be shop
    manager before I knew it. You know your place is
    too small for you ever to offer me that. So I'm
    going to have to give you notice that in a month
    I'll be leaving Tri-X Motors and going over to
    Elite. I really want to thank you guys for all
    you've done for me. You know, you can count on me
    whenever you need me.

During this stage, writers must put together all they have done during pre-writing and make some sense of it. They may want to write while in the room with you, stopping from time to time to show you what they have accomplished, and you should encourage that. In fact, there are two particular stages at which you might easily intervene: focusing the thesis and organization.

Focusing the Thesis   Because so many writers use the act of writing as a way of working up new ideas, few good papers keep the same thesis throughout the writing process. (Some writers don't even have a thesis until they discover it in writing a first or second draft of a paper.) If your tutee has written a thesis, your discussion should focus on how well it fits the aim and audience. Another question that can help a writer at this point is how "doable" the project is--that is, how much outside research is necessary to defend the thesis and how long the essay or report will have to be. Talk, also, about focusing the thesis: narrowing its scope and limiting its range.

The following dialogue is an example of some ways a tutor helped a student sharpen her thesis. This case involves someone who has not yet written a draft, but has done some looping to discover why he is interested in Jungian theory. He has written what he considers to be a thesis for a twenty-page psychology term paper: "Dreams are an important part of Jungian theory."

Tutor: From what I know of Jung's theories, that's certainly true. I'm sure no one would argue with you. How were you thinking of supporting your thesis?

Tutee: Well, I thought I'd describe Jungian dream theory.

Tutor: You mean all of it? I'm sure Jung has a lot to say and there must also be several long books on that subject alone.

Tutee: So, good! I'll have a lot of information.

Tutor: But how will you cut it down? You don't want to write 300 pages, do you?

Tutee: I sure don't. How could I? I'll just cut stuff out.

Tutor: But can you? Look at your thesis. It says all dreams are important to Jungian theory.

Tutee: Can't I change my thesis?

Tutor: How would you do that?

Tutee: Well, I couldn't say only some dreams are important to Jungian theory. That wouldn't be true. Maybe I should talk about a kind of dream, like children in dreams.

Tutor: What about children in dreams? Can you say something more specific than "important?"

Tutee: Not without more reading. I think I'll take a library break and come back tomorrow. Thanks.

Organization   A thesis can determine the organization of a paper, and organization grows out of ideas and the ways in which writers envision their development. But as we have suggested, aim, and audience also dictate organizational patterns. As a tutor, you might discuss organizational patterns and what they accomplish as a way of helping your writers develop strategies for developing the draft.

In addition to sequential patterns, rhetorical strategies, and modes of analysis, this section provides an extensive discussion of outlining as a working tool, or heuristic, for use during writing.

Sequential Patterns   Many beginning writing courses emphasize narrative, descriptive, and process patterns, since they are useful in themselves and can be incorporated into longer, more complex writing projects. In business and industry, they are often necessary to the development of mechanical specifications, catalogue entries, procedure manuals, and systems analyses. These forms imply certain sequential patterns of development.

A narrative, because it is an event or series of events, occurs in time and is often developed chronologically. The art of drama, the short story, and the novel rest on the interesting use of chronological sequence: students should be aware of such devices related to narrative as in medias res (beginning in the middle of things), the flashback, and framing (as when Dorothy falls asleep only to awake in the land of Oz). A narrative can also be used to develop an argument by example, or to explore cause and effect relationships.

Description is often developed according to a spatial sequence. For example, one might describe a face by writing about hair, forehead, eyebrows, all

39

the way down to chin; one might describe a room by writing about what is on the floors, walls, and ceiling. In business, descriptions can be both highly technical and rigidly specified by format; very precise measurements are often required as well. The nature of these will very much vary according to the audience: a consumer may require one sort of a description of a dress, for example, a buyer still another, while the middleman providing the material will need still a third kind.

Process often combines both narrative and descriptive modes of organization. It may focus on how a piece of machinery works, how a company policy is to be translated into procedures for employees, the various stages in a financial cycle, how a dish is cooked or how an experiment is performed. Since people often write out these processes so that they can be followed or duplicated (such as a recipe, experiment, or construction or reconstruction of equipment at a distant site) and used as aids to insure that something functions smoothly (making a repair, solving a problem, or assuring the proper authorization), the need for clarity, precision, and accuracy in writing about process should be obvious.

Rhetorical Strategies   Sequential patterns of organization have their roots in experience and oral forms of delivery. More complex patterns, currently the focus of many writing courses, reflect more abstract logical processes. Students are often asked to take one rhetorical strategy and use that as the primary basis of development, with the idea that they will master each convention in turn. Yet while some essays are exclusively developed using one particular strategy (and essay test questions are often modeled on one or another of them), most writing that a student or employee will have to do requires using these in effective combinations.

Some commonly used rhetorical strategies are: comparison and contrast, cause and effect, definition and categorization. In writing for business, the former might be incorporated into a proposal seeking to persuade a company to adopt a new plant system or to consider the pros and cons of a new site; it might also be used to assess the company's product in relation to the competition. The second strategy might be related to an analysis (see below) of declining sales or production or of some accident occurring on the site; as such it might be a preliminary to the development of new safeguards or even to new methods and programs. The last strategy might be involved in the development of new products or services for the company (what is it that we do now; how would it be sensible for us to expand?).

Modes of Analysis   Analysis demands a most abstract level of thinking: an analytic essay organization involves splitting something into its component parts and discussing the parts; it also involves thinking at highly symbolic and abstract levels. Needless to say, a writer must know a subject rather well before conducting an analysis of it. An analysis of a novel in a literature course, for example, requires that the students have an understanding of what are considered the basic categories of plot, character, theme, style, form (or structure). They must also be thoroughly familiar with the text of the particular novel they are writing about; they should re-read the entire book or selected passages. An analysis of an institution or community may require a knowledge of basic sociological concepts. In addition, various theories are often necessary tools of analysis: thus one may analyze the 1981 recession or the literary production of the 1890's using marxist theory.

Technical Writing Formats   Technical writing-- lab and clinical reports, brochures, catalogue descriptions, technical specifications, formal summaries and proposals--is sometimes considered "non-rhetorical"; theoretically, it is not intended to "persuade." Practically, however, the technical writer must at least "convince" the reader of the accuracy of his or her description or findings and beyond that, provide the necessary support for the acceptance of an hypothesis or set of recommendations. This must also be done in a manner that is clearly accessible to a busy reader, sometimes one outside the field. To help ensure objectivity and readability, company policies and manuals as well as technical and professional organizations, programs and courses emphasize set formats. These model formats aid consistency and predictability and contribute to clarity. (All of these elements reflect the writer's reliability as well as that of the company for which he or she is writing; they also confirm the objectivity of the discipline.) Some formats require that the most general information be supplied first, with increasing levels of specificity or technical data clearly set apart following the general information; another format may require set specifications (as for catalogue descriptions which, for example, include: model number, style description, type, fabrics or ingredients, colors, size, and cost). In nursing, completing an admission history of a client is the first step in nursing that client; it must be documented by the following:

Assessment -- including basis of data and compari-
           son with clinical/diagnostic stan-
           dards
(Nursing) Diagnosis -- with alterations in need
                       related to biophysical and
                       psychosocial factors stated
                       in order of priority
Client Objectives -- both short-term and long-term
                     with related criteria for
                     evaluation
(Nursing Interven-
tions and Rationale -- with documentation of
                       source for each proposed
                       intervention
Evaluation -- of both nursing interventions and
              client's progress toward goals*

A final example of a technical report format widely
used for scientific and social scientific journal
articles and in experimental lab reports often has
the following order:

   a.   Abstract
   b.   Introduction
   c.   Method
   d.   Results
   e.   Discussion
   f.   Conclusion

The abstract indicates the basis of the paper or summary of its findings; the introduction might review
previous research and the motive for and hypothesis
of this article (or the research or experiment covered
by it); the methods must provide the materials and
conditions of the experiment; the results indicate
the outcome and evidence for support of the hypothesis, while the discussion explores possible reasons
for the findings. The conclusion once again summa-
rizes, often indicating suggestions for further work.

Outlining Given all the other strategies available
during the pre-writing and writing stages, outlining
may seem redundant. But for some writers, this strategy may be extremely helpful--by itself or in con-
junction with other techniques.

----
   * This is taken from an actual assignment given in
the School of Nursing, College of New Rochelle, New
Rochelle, New York.

An outline used to help writers plan the organization and development of their writing is a working outline. It should be as concrete as possible, using topic words, phrases, and sentences to help the writer focus on the form the writing will take. Most people think of outlines as strait jackets into which they must fit their essays, rather than as forms which can help them find the "shape" of their ideas. Once the student has a sense of the form, he or she should be able to develop the content more easily.

Model of a Working Outline   For example, your tutee has been asked to write an extended essay for a world drama course. Among several topics suggested by the teacher, the student has chosen to trace a tradition, i.e., show how a playwright reads and consciously reshapes the work of a predecessor. The student has come far in deciding on the overall theme of the paper; in discussion you might begin by choosing two plays which suggest some sort of comparison: The Stronger by August Strindberg, let us say, and Hughie by Eugene O'Neill. Following the tutor's suggestion, the student uses an outline form that will stimulate or contrast strategies of development as follows:

	The Stronger	Hughie
structure	one act "dramatic monologue"	one act primarily monologue minimal dialogue (remedies problem of totally silent character)
character	two characters on stage (discounting maid walk-on) one character off-stage	two characters on stage one (or two?) characters off-stage
setting	inn (European)	hotel (lobby) (American)
content	marriage/deceit explicit triad	implicit triad and rivalry subsumed under friendship
theme	disillusion: revelation (of obj. truth) thru the reflection of a silent other	illusion: self-revelation
"evidence" of relationship (influence)	theoretical (poetic theory of influence) structuralism also Bloom	historical Ck. Letters? Journals?

Notice that the outline helps to insure that the writer will consider parallel elements. When the student came to examine the relationship between the two writers, she recognized that beyond analytical links she had no evidence that a comparison between Strindberg and O'Neill was justified by reality. A case might be made historically only for Strindberg's influence on O'Neill. That pointed her to the need for research and clarified what the focus of the research might be. However, she left a blank in column one, which alerted her that the "equation" was not reversible (Strindberg wasn't influenced by O'Neill) and so she discussed it with her instructor who suggested that our interpretations of older figures are very much affected by the work of more recent writers who have been influenced by them, that is, our interpretations of Strindberg are, in part, contingent on what we know of O'Neill's plays. This so-called structuralist theory is ahistorical and therefore parallel to historical evidence indicated in column two in that it, too, shows a relationship between the two writers. The writer then filled in column one noting further research to be done there. Certainly the student will now be able to use the scheme for a draft, in which she develops the points listed under each category from the point of view of her thesis: The Mutual Admiration of Strindberg and O'Neill.

Other Sample Working Outlines   Here are some sample outlines developed for specific essays:

Narration: Travel in China
Beginning: Preparation
Middle: Touring Peking
Climax: Meeting an American Friend
Denouement: Dining with Chinese friends
End: Departure

Argument: A Proposal to Ban Animals from Urban Locations - Apartments
Proof 1: Animals have no room to exercise.
Proof 2: The apartment tends to smell.
Proof 3: Animals can invade the privacy of neighbors with their barking or meowing.

Process: The Fibonacci Sequence
One: Record the initial number, 1.
Two: Add a second number, which is the sum of numbers in order = 1.
Three: Add third number = 2, which is the sum of the last two digits in sequential order.
Four: Add fourth number = 3, which is, also, the sum of the last two digits of the order.
Five: Add fifth number - 5, which is, again, the sum of the last two digits (2, 3), and so on.

The writer of this outline must write an extended paragraph for her math course. After the tutee recorded this process outline, the tutor reflected on the repetitive explanations in steps 3, 4, and 5. "Will the last addition to the sequence always be the sum of the previous two digits?" she asked. The student writer could then see that an introductory generalization would be an informative guideline and began the essay with: "The Fibonacci sequence is a sequence developed by addition, specifically the combination of any two consecutive numbers." The tutor then asked if the "and so on" was necessary. The writer decided that the explanation should display the sequence at each step and display the entire sequence at the end by way of summary. So she inserted the sequence between each step, after step two, showing 1, 1; after step three 1, 1, 2, and ending with: "The entire sequence would then look like this: 1, 1, 2, 3, 5, 8, 21, 34, 55....."*

Cause and Effect (As part of a company proposal to revise personnel sick-pay policies)
immediate cause: policy whereby accumulated sick leave expires at five-year intervals
short-term effect: 22% increase of personnel requesting sick leave over 1984
long-term effect: cyclical fall-offs of productivity out of sync with production schedules
direct consequence: 45% decrease in project completion
indirect result: failure to obtain federal renewal

In addition, outlines may also be useful after the first draft of a paper has been written. If the essay follows a particular rhetorical model, schematizing it may allow a writer to see the blanks in the paper's development.

The Essay Map   Sample Essay Map: San Francisco
I love San Francisco. The waterfront is always exciting (and delicious). The views atop the hills are thrilling. Finally the streets, dotted with charming Victorian houses and newer restaurants and boutiques, are always a pleasure to walk.

---

* This is derived from Janis Forman, "Notes Toward Writing Across the Curriculum, " Journal of Basic Writing: Reinforcement 2, 4 (Spring/Summer 1980), pp. 14-15.

V. REVISION

Revising can either be viewed as the last stage of the composing process or a separate stage that follows composing. However it is viewed, it involves reorganizing and the pruning and perfecting of style, syntax, and grammar, a process which requires the skill of looking at a paper objectively. What follows are techniques for enabling your tutee to gain perspective on a paper so that he or she can then make necessary changes. The Peer Critique and Self-Critique give writers some ways to "see" what they've done in the first draft(s) so they can figure out how to improve it.

Peer Critiques

In peer critiquing, writers act as each other's critics. With practice, they will learn to be good critics; in fact, they will probably find it easier to critique each other's papers than to critique their own because they will have more distance from another's paper and be more objective. Discussion of these critiques, with each other and with you, will help them reinforce their revising skills so they can then transfer these skills to their own work.

<u>Structure</u>   Peer-critiquing takes at least two people. In a work situation, people will naturally call on people in their own department or on other colleagues; or the writing "context" will establish "natural" readers, people involved in the project. In a tutorial group, you can pair two people, if there is an even number, dividing them in pairs and having them exchange papers. With an odd-numbered group, you can ask members to pass their papers to the person on their right so that no one is critiquing the paper of the person who is critiquing him or her. Your criteria for choosing a structure will depend on the number of people you are working with, their skills' level, and, generally, how well they get along. (You don't want two people who hate each other to critique each other's papers.)

The Writing Critique   After tutees have papers to critique you need to give them guidelines to follow. Without these guidelines, the critiquing session could turn into a mutual "stroking" session, each student being fearful of hurting the other's feelings or not knowing what to look for. On the other hand, it could turn into a free-for-all, negative criticism replacing judicious evaluation.

Kenneth A. Bruffee in his Short Course in Writing, suggests that writing critics begin the critiquing process by learning to describe accurately a piece of writing before they evaluate it. He asks peer critics to find the main idea and then describe how the paper is developed; once they have done this with a few papers, they go on to evaluate the paper for such aspects as unity, coherence, clarity, organization, mechanics and style. All this is done in a supportive way; peer-critics evaluate the strengths of the essay and tell how a draft can be improved.

Another method, one possibly more valuable for basic writers, asks for very definite criteria: does the essay have a main idea which states the subject of the essay and an opinion of the subject; does the body have examples, illustrations, facts, and/or explanations? Is the body of the essay clearly related to the thesis? Does the essay have a conclusion? How many mechanical errors does the essay have?

Of course, if the writing assignment has specific requirements, you can add these to the criteria; for example, if the writer is filing a grievance, the facts of the case must be clearly stated as well as the manner of redress the writer is requesting. When you have decided what you want writers to look for in the critique--and what is best suited to the level of their own development and to their current writing needs--you should develop your own critique.

Practice Activity

Following is a writing sample and a completed critique for it. Complete the blank critique, before reviewing the sample critique which follows. (Besides using the blank to see how a critique "works," you may also wish to use it as you begin to develop your own.)

47

Mrs. Gordon

1 I am a speed typist. I can type over 100 words a minute on a bad day, 125 and over when I'm in top form. I worked my way through under-graduate school typing at night and on weekends. I was paid by the letter and would sit, hunched over the IBM, earphones plugged in my ears, watching the digits of the lettercounter clock up my A.A. and my B.A. and sometimes when I picked up my check, I would say a belated thank you to my highschool typing teacher, Mrs. Gordon.

2 I was a shy kid: unhappy, quiet, and, at sixteen, rather defeated. My sister preceded me in highschool by three years. She was the opposite: gorgeous, popular, a favorite of teachers and students alike. The teachers never ceased to remind me about the difference between us. "How strange," they would say. "You're so different, you two." At the time I thought they were being kind. Different was their word for inferior, wretched, a DRIP. I suffered through my classes in her shadow. I was smart, but who cared? I wasn't pretty, or popular, and in the honors' classes there were lots of smarties. Everyone expected me to be smart and no one paid particular attention to anything I did. Being smart didn't get me dates, or votes, or friends. My studies didn't

exactly suffer. My performance was adequate. However, I was always unhappy. School was tedious and boring. I saw no reason to read, write, or study.

3 I took typing in my junior year in highschool, mainly because my mother urged me to. "Type and you'll never starve." she said. I complied. It didn't much matter anyway; since it was a minor course, it didn't count in my average, I could do badly and it wouldn't matter. So I sat there for two weeks, never speaking, lethargically, going through the drills, making many mistakes.

4 One day, in the middle of a BIG quiz, Mrs. Gordon came up to me, put her hand on my shoulder and asked me to stop for a minute. She was a young woman and when I looked up at her I realized she wasn't more than 21 or 22. She approached me like a friend. She asked me why I wasn't putting more into my work. "You should be doing better," she said. I never knew why she had singled me out for that pronouncement but it performed some kind of miracle for me. By mid-term I was typing 50 WPM and by the final 80. I was the star of the class, twice as fast as anyone else. In fact, I won the typing medal for the entire school.

5 I have changed much since then and many fine things have made me feel good about myself. But I still find that experience to be the high point of my education. For Mrs. Gordon was the first teacher who

cared enough to expect something special from me.   In striving not to disappoint her, I discovered I had special gifts, different from my sister's but no less special.   As a mother this has served me well.   For I learned that everyone is different, and they must be allowed to be different or they may never find out who they really are.

The Writing Critique

1. <u>Describe</u> the essay (do not evaluate it).

   a. What is the essay trying to say (its aim)? (See if you can find a sentence that gives the main point).

   b. How does the essay develop its thesis? (What proofs does the writer offer to convince the reader? What details does he or she include?)

   c. What audience is this essay directed towards? (Why do you say this? Select words and phrases which suggest audience.)

   d. What is the voice of this essay? Note key words and phrases.

51

2. Now <u>evaluate</u> the essay.

    a. Is the essay unified and coherent? (Do the
        thesis and main ideas relate logically? Does
        everything agree with the main point?)

    b. Are the ideas developed thoroughly? Are they
        convincing? (If the answer is no, explain.)

    c. Is the audience and voice appropriate? (Why
        or why not?)

3. Is the style clear, interesting, aesthetic? How
    can it be improved? (Note at least two interest-
    ing words, phrases, etc.)

4. Are the mechanics (grammar, punctuation, spelling)
    correct? Note specific problems.

The Writing Critique

1. <u>Describe</u> the essay (do not evaluate it).

    a. What is the essay trying to say (its aim)?
        (See if you can find a sentence that gives
        the main point).

    *She has a lot to thank Mrs. Gordon for.
    (what a difference a small incident can
    make in somebody's life)
    (No sentence gives main point.)*

    b. How does the essay develop its thesis? (What
        proofs does the writer offer to convince the
        reader? What details does he or she include?)

    *#1: introd. to writer of paper : student
    her way through school by typing
    #2: shy kid : compares herself to sister and
    comes out worse
    #3 : takes typing course, doesn't do well
    #4 : Mrs. Gordon gave her encouragement*

    c. What audience is this essay directed towards?
        (Why do you say this? Select words and
        phrases which suggest audience.)

    *fellow students in writing class ?
    other women (who've felt like
    the little sister) or anyone whose
    experienced the awful self-concern
    of adolescence*

    d. What is the voice of this essay? Note key
        words and phrases.

    intimate, self-pitying

2. Now <u>evaluate</u> the essay.

    a. Is the essay unified and coherent? (Do the
        thesis and main ideas relate logically? Does
        everything agree with the main point?)

        *Mostly, altho' the conclusion took me by sur-
        prise. I'm not sure why it's there - it seems
        tagged on and needs lots more explanation
        if it's really going to come off. The writer
        comes back to herself when I expected her
        to talk more about the Mrs. Gordons of the world.*

    b. Are the ideas developed thoroughly? Are they
        convincing? (If the answer is no, explain.)

        *See above: if she's going to focus on her own
        development, maybe she should change the
        title and write giving more details on how
        this affected her life (and the lives of her
        children). How is she using all she learned?
        If she's going to focus on Mrs. Gordon, she should
        develop ideas on education, the imp. of personal
        caring.*

    c. Is the audience and voice appropriate? (Why
        or why not?)

        *Voice should be more ironic, or funnier. She knows
        better now and self-pity does not make
        the reader sympathetic, only impatient.*

3. Is the style clear, interesting, aesthetic? How
    can it be improved? (Note at least two interest-
    ing words, phrases, etc.) *Plain: clear but
    somewhat dull. I liked the use of dialogue
    and quotations, the image in the first # (it
    reminded me of cartoons where you see dollar
    signs flashing in people's eyes) and the way she
    set up parallel structures for comparison with
    her sister in # 2. Favorite sentence: "Different was*

4. Are the mechanics (grammar, punctuation, spelling)
    correct? Note specific problems. *their word for
    inferior, wretched,
    a DRIP."*

        *mechanics good
        #1 - undergraduate - no hyphen
        #3 - high school - 2 words
            - no comma after lethargically*

<u>Procedure</u> Once students have paper guidelines, they are ready to critique. Depending on your particular tutoring situation, your writers may do their critiques at home, on the job, or at the center. What is important is that they have adequate time and that the critique is written--a written critique will be much more specific and well thought out than one delivered orally. (Such writing also provides additional practice in developing analytical skill.)

Discussion about critiques can take place in a number of ways. Pairs can sit by themselves and read their critiques out loud. An odd-numbered group, or a group of two pairs can do a group critique in which the writer reads his or her paper aloud, the critiquer reads his or her critique, and the group joins in, agreeing and disagreeing where appropriate. You, as tutor, should try to sit in during initial critiquing efforts; however, once students become more practiced at peer-critiquing, they do best without your continuous presence. Thus, they can develop a sense of independence and authority that will help them critique themselves when they write outside of the tutorial.

The Self-Critique

Having mastered the peer critique, that is, being able to describe and evaluate the writing of others with objectivity, writers can often use the critique-- and their enhanced distance--to look at and assess their own work. They should be able to use the critique for themselves, to determine whether they have met their original goals and to begin revising. To encourage this, have tutees write as much of the critique on their own as they are able. If you or your tutee do not have the time or inclination to write up the critique, you may use the form as a guide for discussing the writer's work, nonetheless.

Revision Trouble-Shooting

The scope of this book does not allow for us to examine all the possible problems your tutees may have during writing. The following areas are those that tend to present the most difficulty.

Thesis and Organization   Although some professional writing does not have a thesis sentence per se, the thesis being implied, beginning writers should be encouraged to have such a sentence or group of sentences, so that they are aware of what they are trying to say at all times. In fact, if they underline this sentence they will have an even better chance of remembering it. It is often at the revision stage, when ideas are changing and getting remodelled, that the thesis gets lost--that is, ideas go off the track, developed for their own sakes and not for how they will fit in with the thesis. These new ideas may well point to another thesis entirely. The writer must be aware of this and work with it.

Changes in thesis will in turn affect the organization and the tutor may wish to restructure his or her paper accordingly. At this stage you may want to show the writer examples of how the thesis gets changed in the draft process by showing examples of drafts you or your past tutees have written.

Coherence   Since coherence refers to the smooth and logical connections between ideas, it is very difficult for beginning writers to spot incoherence in their own work. Coherence is established in a variety of ways: through syntax (coordination and subordination); through transitional phrases and expressions; through the qualifications and modifications of an idea, and through repetition and variation. Some phrases and expressions emerge naturally from the organizational pattern the writer uses, and you can alert your student to these, and connect them to the patterns from which they flow by providing lists of phrases and expressions appropriate to the assignment. If you are reviewing a draft, you may use an arrow or arc between two sentences and ask the writer to talk out the connection. The challenge to the writer is always to make explicit the relationship between ideas within sentences, between sentences, and between paragraphs. To give your students practice, you might also create exercises like the one on the next page.

Insert transitional phrases and expressions, where appropriate, to make the following paragraph clearer and more coherent.

Winter came this morning with a sharp chill. I was prepared. The first gust found me bundled in goosedown elegance. I was wrapped up snuggly. Many people were chilled to the bone. They hadn't realized that in November, in New York, anything can happen. I didn't care about them. I was warm.

An exercise like the one above will, at the least, make your tutees familiar with transitions and how they are used in writing. Whether or not students can transfer this "exercise knowledge" to their writing remains to be seen. You will increase their chances of using transitional expressions if you make certain your tutees understand the meaning of the words themselves. Lists of similar and related terms new to the writer tend to be confusing to some, and if writers feel more confident about their meaning they will more likely use them.

Development   Very likely your tutee will have to develop some ideas in more detail. The heuristic devices discussed in previous sections should go a long way to helping them find and develop ideas. Following are some other ways to develop a paper, that is support arguments, clarify ideas, and heighten emotional expression in a work of writing.

Facts   Whether or not your tutee is writing a "research" paper (a paper that requires library research), facts are necessary when one writes something controversial and useful in a variety of circumstances so that the essay or report is more believable. (For example, although a person could say Block Island is of historical significance, how much more interesting it would be to describe its first discovery in the early seventeenth century by the Dutch, and its settlement in the late seventeenth century by the English.) Encourage writers to use facts by demystifying the library for them. Take them there and help them find useful information. (This is something you can do with one student much more easily than a teacher can do with an entire class.) Do exercises like the following to help increase their confidence in doing library work:

Library Scavenger Hunt

Find the following information and bring it back to your tutor in an hour.
1. The page numbers of an article entitled "In the Middle of the Road," written by Eugene McCarthy and published in the N.Y. Times Travel Section, Nov. 8, 1981.
2. The author of Childhood's End.
3. The copyright date of Down These Mean Streets, by Piri Thomas.
4. The birthplace and birthdate of Albert Einstein.
5. The Board of Directors of Crocker National Bank.

Your examples, however, should be based on the writer's needs: it is not the purpose of a Scavenger Hunt to send someone on a wild goose chase; it is rather to isolate relevant data which the writer will find useful to incorporate into his or her own paper.

Examples Beginners' papers tend to have many abstract ideas and few examples to back them up, perhaps because the effort expended on coming up with the idea, or rather, getting it down on paper, is so exhausting. That's why the revision stage, when energy is renewed, is such a good time to fill in. Where appropriate, your tutee should be encouraged to use phrases such as for example, or e.g., or for instance.
One way of developing "example awareness" in your tutees is by having them point out instances of examples in actual passages of writing, their own, student, and professional writing. Then ask them to go over other passages with all the examples removed, discussing what kinds of examples they think they need. Finally, see if they can apply what they have learned to their own writing.

Details Much good work has been done with developing the student writer's use of sensory details. Some teachers send students out with cameras to make montages of what they see--visual essays which are then transliterated into a written essay. Another technique has students blindfold themselves and describe sounds; in another they describe in detail a small, unfamiliar object. All these methods hope to develop students' ability to transfer what they see, hear, smell, touch,and taste to their writing.
Any device that allows writers access to their senses may be productive (see "Talking a Story," described under Invention), especially in the revision

stage where the teacher, critiquer, you, or students themselves may have noticed a dryness and lack of vivacity in the writing. But first, student writers should be made aware of the difference between the general and the specific, for without this knowledge they will not be able to locate where details are missing in the first place. For example, "the stuffed bear on the chair" could be any bear, of any color, size, shape, as could the chair. An exercise like the following can help you heighten your tutee's awareness of the importance of detail. It can also be used to show how detail is often conveyed through similes and metaphors.

Identify whether details in the following paragraph are general or specific by circling details and putting a G or S above them. Then rewrite the sentences, making the details more specific.

When I first walked into the room I had the eerie sense I had been there before. The picture over the mantle looked strangely familiar, as did the mahogany, oblong-shaped clock. I knew I had seen the purple rya rug before, and the old couch in the corner. The Victorian wing chairs, stiff and formal like the prudish Queen for whom they were named, were once part of my life. But most familiar was the onyx ball, seamed with swirls of brown and orange, heavy and mysterious like a fortune-telling instrument of old.

Explanations   Explanations are similar to details in that they, too, give additional information. Indeed, an explanation may include many details, facts, and even examples in order to make a complex, potentially confusing, idea more clear.
The need for explanation should be presented at the time you and your tutee discuss audience. For, the degree and nature of explanation is intimately tied to who the reader is. If the reader knows about the subject, fewer and different kinds of explanations will be necessary than if the reader is not knowledgeable. Have your tutee read the essay out loud and you play the audience. Then you can comment at appropriate times saying "huh?" or "what?" when not enough is said, or "yawn" when too much has been explained. (If lab policy does not permit you to look at students' essays before they are handed in, you can try the same device having the student read a poor text, or one from which explanations have been deleted.

59

<u>Stories</u>   Beginning writers are often unaware that
they may use anecdotes in their writing. They think,
mistakenly, that because stories are not dry they have
no place in academic writing. And perhaps stories
should not be used in scholarly essays written for the
academic community or in business writing (although the
point is arguable).. However, many college essays are
not meant for scholars. In fact, many composition
courses are based almost entirely on experiential writing.   Therefore, once propriety has been discussed (in
terms of audience, that is) explore using stories,
personal or otherwise. Reproducing a passage, like
that below, to discuss how a story is used as a means
of development is a good way to begin:

> People always tell you that when you interview for
> a job you should dress professionally. My career
> counselor warned me that if I didn't "shape up"
> that is, wear a tie, dark suit, clean white
> shirt, polished shoes, I wouldn't have a chance of
> getting a job. Well, I showed him. On the plane
> home from college last summer I wore the grungiest
> clothes I had (didn't want to shock my parents by
> looking too neat)--dirty sneakers, a black tee-
> shirt with a silver and gold Rolling Stones decal
> on it, jeans that hadn't been washed in weeks. I
> was seated next to a man in his thirties and, over
> dinner, we started talking. It seemed he was
> interested in computers too. So we talked about
> computers the rest of the trip. As we were about
> to land at San Francisco airport he said, "What
> are you doing this summer?" When I told him I
> would be looking for a job he said, "Want one in
> my company?" It turned out he owned a small com-
> puter business and was, in effect, interviewing me
> during the trip, jeans and all.

<u>Dialogue</u>   Dialogue is similarly underutilized in
writing, because it seems too informal, too "easy."
Yet, once students get the hang of dialogue writing,
many find it enlivens what they say. For dialogue can
be used as example, by way of explanation, in stories,
and to provide vivid and interesting details.
    First, however, students must be taught how to
write dialogue, and some find it difficult. Many
students, for example, have trouble discerning between direct and indirect quotes. Others don't know
what actually belongs in quotation marks--because
they don't understand what quotation marks actually
do. So don't neglect elementary tasks such as having

students copy written dialogue, transpose direct
quotations into indirect quotations, and vice versa,
and transcribe your conversation and their own. Then
they can go on to make up dialogue, differentiate
characters by dialogue, use dialect, etc.

A number of exercises help students develop these
latter skills. For example, you may send writers to
the cafeteria with a pad and paper to copy dialogue
they hear. Or you may create problem situations, like
the one below, in which the written response must
contain dialogue.

Practice Activity

You are in a crowded luncheonette and have 15
minutes to eat. You have just ordered a ham and
cheese sandwich with mustard but instead they brought
it with mayonnaise. You hate mayo. Describe the en-
suing conversation between you and your waiter.

Graphs, Tables, Illustrations   Most technical and
scientific writing must use graphic and tabular material; much writing in business, history, the social
sciences, and art will benefit from such material.
Yet this aspect of writing is often little discussed
or taught. You, then, are in a critical position to
be helpful to writers in getting them to think about
ways in which they can use diagrams, tables, graphs,
and in helping them to master these forms.

Graphs, pictures, diagrams may either supplement
or replace material in the written text; therefore,
they directly affect the readability and the propor-
tions of the paper. Drawings may enhance or replace
verbal descriptions of fabrics, designs, machinery,
chemical reactions. Tables put data into summary form
and graphs illustrate trends; both free the writer to
use less of the paper to explain and more to analyze
and draw conclusions about comparisons, tendencies,
correctness; they also leave the reader freer to follow the writer's reasoning and thinking and to draw
his or her own conclusions about what is being described or argued. Finally, when a difficult or new
idea is introduced, a block diagram or flowchart can
make the theory, process, or function much easier to
understand.

Style   Style is very difficult for a beginning writer to revise unless a more experienced stylist inter-
venes. The tutorial provides such an opportunity:
tutors can work with students on such aspects of style
as passive vs. active voice, paralles construction,
wordiness, sentence length and variation, clarity.

(If lab policy does not permit you to look at un-
graded papers, and if the paper has not yet been seen
by an instructor, your role will be to familiarize
your tutee with the most common stylistic considerations.)

Passive Voice   First, you must explain passive
voice; then you must explain when it is and when it
is not appropriate to use it. While it has been an
extremely popular device in technical writing, the
trend here, too, is toward active or imperative constructions, mainly because active voice is livelier
and more interesting.

Pick any scholarly journal, especially in the
sciences and social sciences, and you will find an
ample number of passages in passive voice. Copy a few
and use some to show writers how to change sentences
in the passive voice to active voice. Writers should
easily see the difference and be able to revise the
rest themselves. Or ask tutees to change active to
passive forms. Then, after they are saturated with
this subject, ask them to look in their own essay for
passive constructions. Note, however, that not all
passive voice deserves changing. It has a use, but
like any stylistic modality, it should be used pur-
posefully to create a particular affect.

Parallel Construction   Once students recognize
their problems with parallel construction, they can
usually quickly eliminate them--probably because
non-parallel constructions sound so clumsy. As with
constructions in the passive voice, writers can best
learn to correct non-parallel constructions by first
looking at other examples; correcting these will help
them eliminate the constructions in their own writing.
Therefore you may wish to develop exercises like the
one below and have writers pick out and correct non-
parallel sentences before asking writers to check
their own essays.

Practice Activity

Rewrite the following sentences to make them
parallel.
    1. The dog likes barking, eating, scratching, and
to roll down hills.
    2. There are four sports that I do well: skiing,
bowling, and to hike and camp.
    3. To be a good typist you need to sit up
straight and curving your fingers; learning the key-
board helps, too.

Wordiness   Wordiness is often the last stylistic
fault writers learn to eliminate and the guiltiest
writers may be those who pride themselves on using
"technical" prose and the jargon that has often con-
stituted (and still constitutes) the tools of the
technical trade. The best way to get rid of wordiness
is to read incisive crisp prose by expert writers, to
become aware of how it sounds, and to work at paring
extraneous words and expressions--filler phrases and
"bull" sentences that do not explain or forward what
is being said. To do this, the writer should work
closely with an editor on the paper in question, on
other work the writer has done, or with exercises in
style manuals devoted to developing incisive writing.
Your students may get discouraged at this stage; they
may feel that their style is hopelessly inadequate.
Try to show them how much the revising stage involves
stylistic editing, how even professional writers do
seven or eight drafts to get the style exact. Talk
about style as craft, developed over time and through
training. Show them drafts you have written. A
sports metaphor is a good one; for while few people
would deny the need to keep in good physical shape in
order to be good athletes, they do not see the same
need in writing. And they should. Smooth flow, clear
word choice, lively expression all come from prac-
tice--continual practice. And that means revision.
However, remember to show them ways to fill the empty
spaces created when they eliminate wordiness or else
they may still feel it is better to be wordy than to
write too little. Besides, if your tutees have gone
through the composing process as described before
and used the prewriting strategies and strategies of
invention, they will have had the pleasure of discov-
ering that they have many significant things to say.

Clarity   When we refer to clarity during the revision stage we are referring to word choice. (Other
kinds of imprecisions are discussed under development.) Imprecise or unclear word choice is very common among novice writers. Often they feel they have
to impress when writing, and thus use words they are
not really comfortable with; or they may have a limited vocabulary, and when seeking the "right" word,
look to a dictionary or thesaurus; or they may have
mislearned a word.
However, clarity is an ideal that often varies
with audience and aim. Technical terminology and
specifications may make clear to the engineer or the
architect what it obscures for the builder or carpen-
ter; a doctor is required to use certain jargon in
writing for his colleagues that would be unthinkable
in a document for patients. While in theory a clear,
plain style is favored, in practice word choices are

often made to reveal the writer's knowledge of, and adherence to the code of a particular group or discipline, much the same way that writers conform to certain formats in their presentations.

Your role as a tutor, then, is to:

- insure that the writer is using technical jargon in a technically correct sense and eliminating it when it serves no real purpose;

- teach your tutee to use a thesaurus properly and give him or her practice using it;

- point out when the student misuses a word in conversation;

- encourage your tutees to keep a list of misused words with their proper meaning and an example of their correct use in a sentence;

- explain difficult vocabulary;

- encourage students to discuss unfamiliar words in readings.

In other words, the only way to learn vocabulary is actively to use words and to become comfortable with them.

Sentence Length, Variety, and Verve   Above all, writers must be interesting. If everything else we have talked about works, but if the sentences are all the same kind and length, the writing will sound ugly and be boring--albeit "correct." Several techniques have been developed to liven up syntax; we will highlight sentence combining and style analysis.

Sentence Combining was developed to improve writers' syntactical fluency, that is, their ability to expand on their ideas within sentences, using subordinators, coordinators, and various kinds of phrases to vary sentence patterns. Beginning writers, afraid to expand on their ideas within a sentence and make possible errors, tend to write in simple sentences. Sentence combining gets them to expand their sentences by asking them to combine sentences and join them with conjunctions. For example, "I went to the store. I wanted some candy." is combined to become "I went to the store because I wanted some candy." Combining the sentences not only made the combined sentence more interesting, but showed an important relationship between the two simple ideas.

To give your tutees practice in sentence combining, you can make up your sentences, or you can use material in textbooks (see bibliography). The advantage of using textbook material is that it is designed developmentally and might prove valuable

64

in helping students build the skills they need to construct more stylistically sophisticated paragraphs and essays.

Style Analysis asks students to copy passages written by good professional writers and then to try to find out what is unique about the writing. The idea behind style analysis is that by analysing the style of others, students will be able to transfer what they learned about style to their own writing. A variation of this, although one that demands a degree of skill and practice, takes students a step further and asks them to actually mimic the professional writer's style. They can do this by leaving in word constructions and replacing words, for example Joyce writes in "Araby": "North Richmond Street, being blind, was a quiet street, except at the hour when the Christian Brothers' School set the boys free." Mimicking that, you might write, "My niece, being vain, was a boring child, except when she went swimming and forgot all about herself."

VI. TUTORING MECHANICS: GRAMMAR, PUNCTUATION, SPELLING AND FORMAT

Mechanics has been left for last not because it is deemed less important than anything else in writing; indeed, faulty grammar and spelling can mar a writer's style, while improper punctuation can smudge the clarity and impede the development of a piece of writing. We believe, however, that mechanics should be the last thing your tutee looks for--so that, in contrast to traditional writing pedagogy, a concern with grammar does not obstruct the flow of ideas in the early stages of writing. All the same, mechanics is a concern, a very real concern in recent years, and you should help writers at this final stage understand why and how it is important.

May we suggest all writing tutors read Mina Shaughnessy's Errors and Expectations before beginning any work with writers on grammar. It resulted from years of research and study of student writing and is the single most comprehensive book on the mechanical (and not so mechanical) errors of basic writers and how to help students deal with them. Her main point, stressed again and again (and by us as well), is that first, before you do any work correcting errors, you must help your tutees understand the reasons they are making the kinds of errors they are making. Once they know the reason for the error, they will be able to fix it. More important, they won't see their mistakes as a result of stupidity.

As a beginning tutor, you are probably not an expert in grammar. No one expects you to be; you are, however, expected to admit what you don't know and carefully check what you think you do know. You should be working on your grammar continually: reading, doing exercises, talking to other tutors and teachers. You should know what books to go to when you don't have an explanation at your fingertips; like when you need to discuss the difference between a participle and a gerund. Most important, you should not be afraid to ask for help. Calling another tutor or an instructor over to explain or verify a point should not diminish your tutee's confidence in you if you generally show an understanding of writing and a sincere desire to help. False information and posturing will more surely undermine you and your tutee's relationship. Following are productive things you can do.

Error Chart

Encourage your tutees to keep a record, by category, of the errors they make in each paper and the context in which they are made. Then ask them to correct the errors (including spelling mistakes). By doing this, your tutees not only isolate the errors corrected but, if they keep the record systematically as a chart, they can assess themselves. They can then see by themselves where they need work. They will also be able to gauge their progress on the chart, noting when they are making fewer errors and when some kinds disappear altogether.

Error Chart: Sample Page

Date	Subject-Verb Agreement	
9/23	Original:	John and Sue was in town today.
	Correction:	John and Sue were in town today.
9/30	Original:	Nobody like to lose all the time.
	Correction:	Nobody likes to lose all the time.
	etc.	

Drill

Although mechanical, there is evidence that drills do work to correct those kinds of problems caused by mislearned patterns. They allow people to memorize new patterns on a basic level so they can train themselves to use the correct material automatically in their writing. Conjugation of verbs, for example, is well taught by drill, as are homophones, names of conjunctions, etc. (See The Tutor Book for discussion of drills.)

Exercises

As we discussed in Chapter 4 of <u>The Tutor Book</u>, exercises differ from drills in that they do not ask for an automatic response. One must think and respond to a question on the basis of material read or presented. You can get exercises from any grammar book.

Or, if these are not available, or interesting, you can make them up yourself on the basis of the material you are trying to teach. If, for example, you are tutoring <u>subjects and verbs</u> you might write or take a paragraph out of a magazine and have the student identify the subjects and verbs in each sentence. Or you might make up sentences similar to the ones the students did incorrectly. Then, when they go over their papers they should find the correction process an easier one. There is one caveat concerning exercises, however. There does not appear to be much carryover from exercises to writing; students doing well on exercises do not learn the material unless they practice it--that is, use what they learned by actually writing. So don't rely too much on exercises and make certain each tutoring session gives students practice in <u>applying</u> what they learned.

Programmed Grammar

There are many good arguments for using programmed grammar. It is designed "scientifically," to teach students to teach themselves. Based on the behavioral theory of Skinner and others, these grammar texts (available also on tape and computer), allow students to go forward only if they have learned the material. Many students prefer working alone and really respond well to these texts; however, whether or not your tutee is one of these students, you should frequently check the student's work. Sometimes students don't understand written explanations in material and are stopped from going further. Some programmed texts don't have enough exercises in areas in which students need extra help. In other words, make certain tutees are getting the one-to-one attention the tutorial should allow.

68

Dictation

Dictation is a good way for students to see if they can correctly write what they hear. If you dictate a paragraph with many homophones, tutees will be able to tell whether they know the difference between or among the homophones when they go over the dictation. Knowledge of how to write dialogue and use quotation can be checked by dictations. Punctuation can be practiced in dictation. Dictations give students a chance to copy correct syntax and, thus, to practice word structures they may not otherwise attempt.

Controlled Composition

Controlled compositions allow students to practice correcting one particular aspect of grammar or structure in context. To do a controlled composition, students are asked to copy a passage, changing a grammatical or structural part of it. In the passage below, written for students who need practice in tense, we ask students to change <u>today</u> to <u>yesterday</u>, making other changes which inevitably follow as a result of the shift in tense.

> Today I will go shopping. I need all sorts of things for the fall, so I will have to get an early start. First I wanted to buy some shoes. I need boots, formal and informal. I can also use a pair of fancy dress shoes. Then I must get some business clothes; that means suits, blouses, and accessories. Finally, I need a coat. I can't afford an expensive coat, fur or down, so I'll probably buy a plain wool coat and, perhaps, dress it up with a scarf or hat. When I finish I will have spent my next five paychecks.

Games

We discussed games in Chapter 4 of The Tutor Book and we would only add here that writing games do exist and some of them, like Word Rummy and Scrabble, are quite effective in teaching students aspects of grammar and, generally, in getting them interested in etymology.

Proofreading

After everything else, you must encourage your student to proofread. When we speak of proofreading, we mean the final reading that the essay gets, after all revisions, when little substantive is changed: some remaining grammatical errors, spelling, style, word choice, typos.

Usually this process takes place after the paper is already typed, so the first things you should discuss with your tutee is how to correct neatly, with white-out, or ink, if permissible, and how to use basic editing like the caret for inserts, the delete sign, the paragraph sign, and the reversal sign for transposing letters, words or even paragraphs. See any standard dictionary for a complete list and make your students aware that dictionaries may be used for editorial reference purposes. What next? If students have kept an error chart, they should glance at it to ascertain where their biggest problems were. That will show them what to look for. Then they should do one or more of a number of things:

- Have you, or, if at home, a friend, read a xerox of the essay slowly while the tutee corrects;

- read their essay slowly into a tape recorder and play the tape back while they correct;

- get heavy paper and cover all but one line, moving the card slowly down as they read;

- read from back to front, starting with the last word of the essay;

- let the paper cool off, preferably overnight

or longer, before proofreading it, so that
they can be more objective about finding
their errors.

A good way of practicing proofreading between
essays is to give students sample paragraphs laden
with the kinds of errors they tend to make. Then tell
them the number and/or type of errors there are.
(This will give them an objective goal.) The one below was prepared for students having trouble with
run-on and comma-splice sentences; however, you can
prepare a similar proofreading essay for any kind of
grammatical or stylistic error.

Practice Activity

Instructions: try to find the errors in the essay
below and correct them. Comma-splices: 5 Run-ons: 3

On Sunday mornings I tend to get a slow start, I
get up late, at the earliest, 11:00 a.m., and then
drag myself from bed. I throw some water on my face
then I stumble out to the kitchen. Once in the kitch-
en, I try to find the coffee pot, this is difficult
because my eyes are barely open, however, eventually
I succeed. Next, I look for the coffee and, once
finding it, measure out the requisite number of cups,
needless to say, I usually get more of the coffee on
the counter than in the pot. Finally I pour in the
water and turn on the fire, and would you believe it,
I turn water into coffee, nearly sleepwalking all the
while.
My next project is to make some eggs, imagine
making eggs when half asleep, it's not easy. Well, I
usually drop a few before I get the job done, but
that's okay. My eggs are so good Sunday mornings. I
make excellent omelets I make fantastic poached eggs,
even if I do get a few eggs on the floor.

All these methods of tutoring grammar have ultimately little or no value if they are done outside
the context of writing. Students do not learn grammar for its own sake (unless they plan to be linguists); they learn it so that imperfect knowledge
of it doesn't interfere with their ability to commu-
nicate in writing. Seen in that context, it can be
an enjoyable experience to learn grammar rather than
the punishment it has become for so many.

71

Finishing Touches:
Cover Letters, Tables of Contents, Outlines

    Various works require preliminary and end matter apart from the report or paper itself. These are intended for the reader rather than the writer, and so students should prepare them after completing the writing process. Preliminary material may involve transmittal sheets, memos, a cover page, table of contents, a list of tables and illustrations that help define the scope of the work and make that immediately apparent to the reader. End matter includes appendices and bibliography. Be sure that your tutee knows which of these is required and what style he or she is expected to follow.

    An outline or table of contents written after the revision stage is intended for the reader rather than for the writer. As such it should follow a format (and use the mechanics) with which the reader is presumed to be familiar. In academic work this may be the Harvard Outline (I, II, A., B., 1., 2., a., b., (1), (2), (a), (b); in technical work and business, a numerical outline (1.1.1, 1.1.2, 1.2.1, 1.2.2) is often preferred.

    You, as tutor, should try to help the student become familiar with the required format and indicate the importance of using the proper manual to discover the relevant mechanics.

VII. ANNOTATED BIBLIOGRAPHY

This bibliography pretends neither to be complete nor objective. Instead, it intends to lead you to works--which you may be interested in as a result of your reading in this pamphlet and tutoring in your program--to learn more about language, writing, and the teaching of writing. Special sections on dialect, and sex and language include a discussion of topics omitted in the text but critical to language teaching and learning.

A word about periodicals   The National Council of Teachers of English (NCTE) and its subsidiary Conference on College Composition and Communication (4 C's) regularly feature articles on various aspects of writing in College English and College Composition and Communication which are available by subscription through national headquarters, 1111 Kenyon Road, Urbana, Illinois 61801.

Teaching English in the Two-Year College is available for $5.00 (individual) or $7.00 (institutional) annual subscription check,made payable to East Carolina University and sent to the Department of English, Greenville, North Carolina 27834.

Perhaps the most important resource is the Writing Lab Newsletter, a publication that contains information not only about but by tutors and serves as a national exchange of practices and queries. Available for a $5.00 contribution marked directly to its editor: Muriel Harris, Department of English, Purdue University, West Lafayette, Indiana 47907.

Journals for those working in technological fields and industry include:

Journal of Engineering Education
Technical Communication
Journal of Technical Writing and Communication
The Technical Writing Teacher
Journal of Business Communication

Arthur, Rosemarie. "The Student-Teacher Conference." College Composition and Communication, 28, No. 4 (December 1977), pp. 338-342. Lays down guidelines, with which tutors will be familiar, about the importance of setting a student at ease, confidentiality, etc., in a one-to-one setting.

Clapp, Oveda, ed. Classroom Practices in Teaching English, 1977-1978: Teaching the Basics-- Really! Urbana, Illinois: National Council of Teachers of English, 1977. A National Council of Teachers of English publication, this collection of essays on teaching, reading, writing, communication, grammar, and literature is directed primarily at the college teacher.

Coles, William E., Jr. The Plural I: The Teaching of Writing. New York: Holt, Rinehart, and Winston, 1978.

Donovan, Timothy and Ben W. McClelland, eds. Teaching Composition. Urbana, Illinois: National Council of Teachers of English, 1979. A variety of essays on composing by some of the best-known writing specialists, this collection of essays reflects current composing theory and its practical application in the college classroom.

Elbow, Peter. Writing With Power: Techniques for Mastering the Writing Process. New York: Oxford University Press, 1981. More strategies for less painful, more productive creating and revising; a follow-up to Elbow's earlier book (below).

Elbow, Peter. Writing Without Teachers. New York: Oxford University Press, 1973. One of the first to emphasize the importance of writing blocks and gamelike and intuitive strategies for getting around them, written in an informed, and often personal, style.

Flower, Linda and John Hayes. "Problem Solving Strategies and the Writing Process." College
English, 39 (December 1977), pp. 449-461. Provides an important list of strategies; useful
for the lab. Shows application of tree diagrams to larger rhetorical forms. (See Chaika
below.)

Hawkins, Thom. Group Inquiry Techniques for Teaching
Writing. Urbana, Ill.: ERIC Clearinghouse
on Reading and Communication Skills/National
Council of Teachers of English, 1976. One of
the leading proponents of peer collaborative
learning offers a theoretical rationale and
specific strategies and tasks. Includes an
evaluation form to be used by group members.

Irmscher, William F. Teaching Expository Writing,
New York: Holt, Rinehart and Winston, 1979.
This book is for beginning teachers of writing
and outlines what Irmscher believes should be
included in a composition class.

Jacobs, Suzanne and Adela Karliner. "Helping Writers
to Think: The Effect of Speech Roles in Individual Conferences on the Quality of Thought."
College English, 38, No. 5 (January 1977),
pp. 489-505. Reinforces the idea of using
tutoring not to "teach" but to enable tutees
to learn.

Klammer, Enno. "Cassettes in the Classroom." College
English, 35 (1973,74), pp. 179-89. Recommends
recording essays with comments: a valuable
idea that tutors can adapt for work with students and which allows students to use cassettes at home to review.

Lanham, Richard. Revising Prose. New York: Charles
Scribner's Sons, 1979. A book that teaches
style by providing numerous exercises on
various aspects of style.

Laque, Carol Feiser and Phyllis A. Sherwood. A Labora-
tory Approach to Writing. Urbana, Illinois:
National Council of Teachers of English, 1977.
Addressed to teachers, this book will, nonetheless, be of interest to tutors for philo-
sophical background and ideas for tutoring,
especially in small groups.

Nash, Thomas. "Effective Pre-Writing Strategies for College Students." (Unpublished Mimeo.) Auburn University, Department of English, n.d. An up-to-date (1981) description of popular pre-writing strategies aimed at the writing tutor and containing sample exercises from current books on the subject.

Ohmann, Richard and W. B. Coley, eds. Ideas for English 101. Urbana, Illinois: National Council of Teachers of English, 1975. Articles on freshman writing by some of the pioneers in composition theory; compiled from issues of College English 1967-1975.

Shor, Ira. Critical Teaching and Everyday Life. Boston: South End Press, 1980. Radical analysis of the composition classroom, it also offers ways of using everyday objects (chairs, hamburgers) as a means of getting writers to think critically about their environment.

Tate, Gary, ed. Teaching Composition: Ten Bibliographical Essays. Fort Worth: Texas Christian University Press, 1976. The distinguished authors of these essays survey the field of composition teaching prior to 1973 and summarize the research on such areas as invention, style, discourse, basic writing, linguistics, and rhetoric.

Trillin, Alice Stewart and Associates. Teaching Basic Skills in College. San Francisco: Jossey-Bass, 1980. This book, written by faculty in reading, writing, ESL, and math at City University of New York, surveys basic skills programs in these areas, detailing how the programs are set up, how students are diagnosed, placed, and instructed.

Evaluation

Cooper, Charles R. and Lee Odell. Evaluating Writing:
    Describing, Measuring, Judging. Urbana, Illi-
    nois: National Council of Teachers of English,
    1977. Discusses different methods at length,
    especially those developed from actual writing.
    One important essay defines the T-unit (main
    clause plus subordinate clauses or modifiers)
    as an important indicator of writing maturity
    (by Kellog Hunt).

McDonald, W.W., Jr. "The Revising Process and the
    Marking of Student Papers." College Composi-
    tion and Communication, 29 (May, 1978), pp.
    167-170. Distinguishes comments that are
    helpful for revising from those that signal a
    "grade." Useful for helping the tutor learn
    what instructors mean and what kinds of com-
    ments and questions tutors might use with stu-
    dents.

Grammar; The Sentence and the Paragraph

Carkeet, David. "Understanding Syntactic Errors in
    Remedial Writing." College English, 38
    (1977), pp. 682-695. Talks about those errors
    that are not grammatical but result in awk-
    wardness and confusion; helpful article for
    the tutor working with intermediate students.

Chaika, Elaine. "Grammars and Teaching." College
    English, 39, No. 7 (March 1978), pp. 770-783.
    Shows usefulness of tree diagrams, especially
    helpful in working on run-ons and fragments.
    Transformational grammar.

Kroll, Barry and John Schafer. "Error-Analysis and the Teaching of Composition." College Composition and Communication, 29, No. 3 (October 1978), pp. 242-248. In the tradition of Shaughnessy (see below), it emphasizes the importance of understanding process over condemning product.

Shaughnessy, Mina. Errors and Expectations: A Guide to Teachers of Writing. New York: Oxford University Press, 1977. This scholar and teacher used the latest in research to examine and discuss the writing of students in her program. Inspiring in its sensitivity and humaneness. Excellent bibliography.

Strong, William. Sentence-Combining: Improving Student Writing Without Formal Grammatical Instruction. Research Report No. 15. Urbana, Illinois: National Council of Teachers of English, 1973. Makes a strong case for sentence combining though other studies have suggested it may not be appropriate to all styles, students, or levels.

"The Uses of Grammar," Journal of Basic Writing, 3 (Spring/Summer 1977) New York: Instructional Resource Center, 1977. A sophisticated discussion of grammars; requires some background. But see Linda Ann Kunz's essay for X-word grammar, a method not discussed by us but which you may wish to apply with writers having trouble with run-ons and fragments.

Whitehall, Harold. Structural Essentials of English. New York: Harcourt, Brace & World, 1956. An easy-to-read, remarkably lucid discussion of one of the new -- structuralist -- grammars and a good introduction to linguistic study: offers insights that might easily be applied in tutoring conjunctions and aspects of punctuation. Short history of the language in appendix.

Aristotle. The Rhetoric and Poetics. Trans. W. Rhys
     Robert and Ingram Bywater. Introd. Fried-
     rich Salmsen. New York: Modern Library,
     1954. The father of us all: Aristotle is the
     first author to define basic principles and
     codify invention, systematize rhetorical
     models, and consider the importance of audi-
     ence.

Becker, A. L. "A Tagmemic Approach to Paragraph Anal-
     ysis." College Composition and Communica-
     tion, 16 (1965), pp. 237-242. Difficult with-
     out a knowledge of linguistic theory.

Britton, James et al. The Development of Writing Abil-
     ities (11-18). Schools Council Research
     Studies. London: Macmillan Education, 1975.
     Reprinted and distributed in paperback by
     National Council of Teachers of English. This
     book shows the process of developing a model
     and definitions for assessment. Includes many
     samples of British students' writing consid-
     ered from the points of view of audience,
     aim, and function.

Christensen, Frances. Notes Toward A New Rhetoric:
     Six Essays for Teachers. New York: Harper &
     Row, 1967. Out of a new generative grammar,
     the author developed a theory of a generative
     rhetoric, so that sentence, paragraph, and
     paper are seen hierarchically and as parallel
     elements. Generalizations show problems of
     using a deductive rather than inductive model.

Cooper, Charles R. and Lee Odell, eds. Research on
     Composing: Points of Departure. Urbana,
     Illinois: National Council of Teachers of
     English, 1978. Provides good summaries and
     comparative discussion of latest theories,
     including Britton, Moffet, Kinneavy.

Corbett, Edward P. J. The Little Rhetoric. New York:
    John Wiley and Sons, 1977. This rhetoric is
    dedicated to Aristotle but also contains the
    fruits of much modern theory on the writing
    process.

D'Angelo, Frank. A Conceptual Theory of Rhetoric.
    Cambridge, Massachusetts: Winthrop, 1975.

Emig, Janet. "Writing as a Mode of Learning." Col-
    lege Composition and Communication, 28 (1977),
    pp. 122-128. One of the earliest articles to
    view the cognitive basis of writing, the
    author is also important for research work in
    the development of syntactical maturity in
    writing (See also, Cooper under Evaluation.)

Hawkins, Thom and Phyllis Brooks, eds. New Directions
    for College Learning Assistance: Improving
    Writing Skills. San Francisco: Jossey-Bass,
    Inc., 1981. This book on writing centers
    includes articles on such topics as lab ad-
    ministration, training tutors, and collabora-
    tive learning. Directed to administrators,
    it also contains several articles by tutors
    themselves.

Hirsch, E. D., Jr. The Philosophy of Composition.
    Chicago: University of Chicago Press, 1977.
    One of the earliest books on composition
    theory and influential in establishing compo-
    sition as a discipline in its own right.

Kaplan, Robert B. "Contrastive Rhetoric and the
    Teaching of Composition." TESOL Quarterly, 1
    (December 1967), pp. 10-16. An article pre-
    ceding Shaughnessy's work (see above) and
    showing how tutoring writing can benefit from
    applied linguistic studies. Useful introduc-
    tory (short) article for the tutor.

Kinneavy, James. A Theory of Discourse. New York:
    W. W. Norton, 1971. Important but often tough-
    going and obscure text which provides a his-
    torical overview of rhetorical theory and an
    exposition of the latest communication theo-
    ries, which include but are not limited to
    writing.

Kinney, James. "Tagmemic Rhetoric: A Reconsideration." College Composition and Communication, 29, No. 2 (May 1978), pp. 141-145. Knowledge of linguistic theory required.

Kneupper, Charles W. "Revising the Tagmemic Heuristic: Theoretical and Pedagogical Considerations." College Composition and Communication, 31,.No. 2 (May 1980), pp. 160-168. For those interested in this theory; background required.

Moffett, James. Teaching the Universe of Discourse. Boston: Houghton-Mifflin, 1968. A student-centered theory of and method for teaching communication skills in grades K-13.

Pitkin, Willis, Jr. "Hierarchies and the Discourse Hierarchy." College English, 38 (March 1977), pp. 648-659. A prelude to the following article.

Pitkin, Willis, Jr. "X/Y: Some Basic Strategies of Discourse." College English, 38 (March 1977), pp. 660-672. In the tradition of Aristotle, the author offers a taxonomy based on more recent theories.

Van Nostrand, A. D. et al. Functional Writing. Boston: Houghton-Mifflin, 1978. Based on mastery learning, this book offers a systematic approach to composition, functioning both as a writing workbook and as a description of the writing process.

Winterowd, W. Ross. Contemporary Rhetoric: A Conceptual Background with Readings. New York: Harcourt Brace Jovanovich, 1975. A difficult but interesting and well-written book which introduces the reader to classical rhetoric and modern theory. Also selections on tagmemic analysis, sentence-combining. Especially good for those interested in aspects of revision: see "The Grammar of Coherence."

Barrass, Robert. Scientists Must Write: A Guide to
    Better Writing for Scientists, Engineers and
    Students. London: Chapman and Hall, 1978.

Cunningham, Donald H. and Herman A. Estrin, eds. The
    Teaching of Technical Writing. Urbana, Illi-
    nois: National Council of Teachers of Eng-
    lish, 1975. Essays which offer definitions
    of technical writing and approaches based on
    them. One essay discusses the results of a
    local survey of industry which gives clear
    evidence of the need for writing skill in the
    workplace (e.g., people at all levels spend
    80% of their jobs concerned with writing.)

Fear, David E. Technical Writing. 2nd ed. New York:
    Random House, 1978. Introductory text useful
    for both students and tutors.

Grossberg, Kathryn Milner. "ERIC/RCS Report: The
    Truth About Technical Writing." English Jour-
    nal, 67, No. 4 (April 1978), pp. 100-102.
    Her review of definitions of technical writing
    lead to the conclusion that it is no different
    from any other kind of writing. Helpful re-
    view of the literature.

Handbook of Technical Writing Practices. 2 Vols.
    eds. Stello Jordan et al. New York: Wiley-
    Interscience, 1971. Reference: An excellent
    anthology by experts in the field, it dis-
    cusses major genres and types, aspects of
    process, and applications of rhetorical and
    discourse theory, along with new trends and
    the impact of technology on communication and
    writing. Series of checklists for outlines,
    rough drafts, final drafts, illustrations,
    and printed publications. Separate chapter
    for annotated bibliography covers encyclope-
    dias, dictionaries, technical reports, busi-
    ness reports, and so on.

Harris, Elizabeth. "Applications of Kinneavy's Theory
    of Discourse to Technical Writing." College
    English, 40, No. 6 (February 1979), pp. 625-
    632. (See Kinneavy above.)

Miller, Carolyn R. "A Humanistic Rationale for Technical Writing." College English, 40, No. 6
(February 1979), pp. 610-617.

Mitchell, Ruth. "Shared Responsibility: Teaching
Technical Writing in the University." College
English, 43, No. 6 (October 1981), pp. 543-
555. Discusses who (English faculty vs. faculty in other disciplines) should and can
teach what; includes discussion of the tutor's
role.

Teaching Scientific Writing. The English Journal, 67,
No. 4 (April 1978). An issue devoted entirely
to the subject.

Dialect

The entries here are merely introductory and focus
primarily on Black Dialect/Language. It was William
A. Stewart who first pointed out that the English of
Blacks should be studied as a coherent system. Other
important researchers (linguists and ethnographers)
who have followed include Americans William Labov,
Raven McDavid, Albert Marckwardt and Roger Shuy and
Britisher Basil Bernstein. Be aware of methodologi-
cal flaws that derive from political and sexist bi-
ases.

Dillard, J. L. Black English: Its History and Usage
in the United States. New York: Random
House, 1973. An important still controversial
study instrumental in helping us understand
the "normal historical factors" that apply to
Black English as much as to other dialects.

Smitherman, Geneva. "'What Go Round Come Round':
King in Perspective." Harvard Education Review, 51 (February 1981), pp. 40-56. The
author discusses implications of King deci-
sion and the question of how a knowledge of
Black English and its social context could
help us to break down language barriers, if
society would permit it. Solid research and
documentation; controversial perspective.

Stoller, Paul, ed. and introd. Black American English: Its Background and Its Usage in the
Schools and in Literature. New York: Dell,
1975. Good introductory anthology, with
readings by several of the authors noted
above.

Tannen, Deborah. "Oral and Literate Strategies in
Discourse." The Linguistics Reporter: A
Newsletter in Applied Linguistics, 22, No. 9
(June 1980), pp. 1-3. Interestingly written
discussion of how oral and written modes af-
fect writing.

Sex and Language

This area is only now being developed as a course of
study and research: without the polemic of feminism,
we would be far less aware of sexual variation and
difference in language. Below are almost the only
texts in existence that summarize careful research
and provide interesting points of departure.

Berryman, Cynthia L. and Virginia A. Eman, eds. Communication, Language and Sex: Proceedings of
the First Annual Conference. Rowley, Massachusetts: Newbury House, 1980. Varied
topics, including the reciprocal influences of
literature and literary criticism, research
perspectives, and implication for, or applications to, classroom instruction.

Kramarae, Cheris. Women and Men Speaking: Frameworks
for Analysis. Rowley, Massachusetts: Newbury
House, 1981. Attempts an interlocking series
of chapters using various social, psychological theories to model their discussions of
language and gender.

Orasanu, Judith, Mariam K. Slater, and Leonora Loeb
    Adler. Language, Sex and Gender: Does 'La
    Difference' Make a Difference? Annals of the
    New York Academy of Sciences, 327. New York:
    Academy of Sciences, 1979. A well-balanced
    series of papers which discuss the relation-
    ships of sex, sexism, language and culture
    from a variety of viewpoints.

Thorn, Barrie and Nancy Henley, eds. Language and
    Sex: Difference and Dominance. Rowley, Massa-
    chusetts: Newbury House, 1975. The initial
    article by the editor provides an excellent
    overview of the research and summary of the
    readings that follow. Essays describe rela-
    tion of sex to topics of discussion, length,
    patterns of intonation, interruption.

Selected Texts

Bruffee, Kenneth A. A Short Course in Writing. 2nd
    ed. Cambridge, Massachusetts: Winthrop,
    1980. This textbook guides the composition
    student through the writing of an essay. It
    includes sections on collaborative learning
    and writing across the curriculum, with a de-
    tailed explanation of peer-critiquing and a
    large selection of student models.

Cowan, Gregory and Elizabeth. Writing. New York:
    John Wiley and Sons, 1980. A composition
    textbook containing many of the latest ap-
    proaches to the teaching of writing. The
    pre-writing section is especially good for
    basic writers. Accompanying workbook may be
    useful in the lab.

Flower, Linda. Problem-Solving Strategies for Writ-
    ing. New York: Harcourt Brace Jovanovich,
    1981.

Gibson, Walker. Seeing and Writing. 2nd ed. New
    York: David McKay, 1974. An excellent col-
    lection of strategies for making prose more
    vivid and fresh. Good exercises in making
    analogies.

Maimon, Elaine P. et al. Writing in the Arts and
      Sciences. Cambridge, Massachusetts: Winth-
      rop, 1981. An important interdisciplinary
      text which discusses study, research, and
      writing skills needed for a variety of disci-
      plines and also takes account of individual
      differences in the writing process. Includes
      a glossary of specialized terms and sample
      student papers in history, sociology, psycho-
      logy, and biology. Excellent for further
      strategies of diagramming and to help the
      tutor working with writers in other fields.

Macrorie, Ken. Telling Writing. Rochelle Park, New
      Jersey: Hayden, 1976. A course in composi-
      tion, written in an informal style and de-
      signed to make student writing more "truth-
      ful." Contains descriptions of free writing,
      the helping aide, and keeping a journal.

Memering, Dean and Frank O'Hare. The Writer's Work.
      Englewood Cliffs, New Jersey: Prentice-Hall,
      1980. Contains many writing samples from stu-
      dent work; good translation of writing process
      for basic writers.

Paull, Michael and Jack Kligerman. Invention: A
      Course in Pre-Writing and Composition. Cam-
      bridge: Winthrop, 1973. One of the ear-
      liest but still relevant texts which combines
      pre-writing strategies -- for developing
      perception through responses to non-representa-
      tional forms and objects -- with composing.
      Some valuable ideas for tutoring.

Raimes, Ann. Focus on Composition. New York: Oxford
      University Press, 1978.

Strong, William. Sentence Combining. New York: Ran-
      dom House, 1973. Based on the research noted
      above, a straightforward series of exercises
      used for practicing sentence complexity and
      variety. Transparencies Masters and Instruc-
      tor's Manual available from the publishers.

Troyka, Lynn Quitman and Jarold Nudelman. Taking Ac-
      tion. Englewood Cliffs, New Jersey: Pren-
      tice-Hall, 1975. A book for developing com-
      munication skills through simulation-gaming.

Wallace, Mary Lewick. "A Bibliography of Programmed
      Texts on English Composition." College Compo-
      sition and Communication, 30 (1979), pp. 58-
      61.

Weiner, Harvey S. The Writing Room: A Resource Book
      for Teachers of English. New York: Oxford
      University Press, 1981. A useful reference
      for the beginning writing teacher containing
      practical advice on all aspects of teaching
      composition. Possible applications to tu-
      toring.